MACMILLAN MUSICALS

*Series Editor: Geoffrey ! a*



# *The Prince and the Pauper*

MUSIC: *Lyndon Jones*

TEXT AND LYRICS: *Mick Loftus*

First performed by Heatham House Youth Theatre,
Twickenham, Middlesex, on 21 March 1983



Macmillan Education

First published 1985

Published by
MACMILLAN EDUCATION LTD
Houndmills, Basingstoke, Hampshire RG21 2XS
and London
Companies and representatives
throughout the world

Typeset by
Wessex Typesetters
Frome, Somerset

Printed in Great Britain by
Vine & Gorfin Ltd, Exmouth, Devon

Cover illustration
by David Dowland
and Joyce Smith

ISBN 0 333 37699 4

## AUTHORS' DEDICATION

This musical was commissioned by David King, Warden of Heatham House Youth Activities Centre, at the suggestion of Keith Hutton who also directed the first production at the Heatham House Youth Theatre, Twickenham, Middlesex, in March 1983. We wish to thank them both for their inspiration and faith in the project.

Also our thanks go to Sandy Gibson and Valerie Loftus for their great help and encouragement during the writing of the show.

Finally, our thanks to the entire cast and backstage crew who brought the script to life, both in England and also on a memorable tour of the USA and Canada.

## INTRODUCTION

This is a full-length show with some twenty-five musical numbers, several of which are quite elaborate and extended. However, the musical language is conventional and the demands for part-singing, for instance, are not beyond the average young singer. In fact, any school or group that can tackle Gilbert and Sullivan or Rodgers and Hammerstein will find this piece well within their grasp.

All parts can be played by young people, though it would probably be more effective if very authoritative figures like Henry VIII and John Canty were played by adults or at least very senior students. Miles Hendon and Hertford also need fairly mature broken voices. The Prince and Tom, who are meant to be identical in appearance, can be played by one person but if there are twins who can do the part(s) obviously this simplifies matters! Actors in the smaller roles can be part of the chorus.

The staging is intended to be very simple with two main lighting areas – one for the poor and one for the rich – and a few significant items of furniture – bench, bed, throne etc. – to set the scene. Costume is important, however. The more realistic and colourful it is the better – money saved on scenery might well go into the hire of at least a few really good period costumes.

The musical accompaniment is for piano, drums and guitar with recorders for the opening march. Recorders and other melody instruments like flute, oboe or violin could be introduced at other points, playing melody lines or counter-melodies with guitar, to vary the accompaniment texture.

## SCENES AND MUSICAL NUMBERS

**Act One**

*Scene 1: The die is cast*

1 Instrumental: 'The Earl of Oxford's march'
2 Chorus: 'The ballad of poverty and plenty' (Full company)
3 Solo: 'Don't turn me away' (Tom)
4 Solo and Chorus: 'If I could see' (Edward, Tom, Beggar, Rich and Poor)
5 Instrumental: 'The Earl of Oxford's march' (Reprise)

*Scene 2: The Prince is mad*

6 Chorus: 'The Prince is mad!' (Hertford, Tom, Jane, Catherine, Fool, Henry, Elizabeth)
7 Solo: 'Have I been too hard on the boy?' (Henry)

*Scene 3: The Prince's troubles begin*

8 Duet: 'No boy of mine' (John, Mrs Canty)
9 Instrumental: 'No boy of mine'/'The Prince is mad!' (Reprise)

*Scene 4: In Westminster Palace*

10 Instrumental: Fanfare
11 Chorus: 'Who do you think you are?' (Hertford, Tom, Catherine, Jane, Henry, Fool, Elizabeth)
12 Instrumental: 'No boy of mine' (Reprise)

*Scene 5: A London street*

*Scene 6: Tom accepts his part*

13 Solo: 'I am no prince' (Tom)
14 Instrumental: 'Make way for the Prince'

*Scene 7: Miles Hendon*

15 'The high cost of living' (Miles)
16 Chorus: 'Make way for Edward, Prince of Wales' (Full company)

## SCENES AND MUSICAL NUMBERS

**Act Two**

*Introduction*
17 Instrumental and Chorus: 'The Earl of Oxford's march'/'Falala' (Rich and Poor)

*Scene 8: Miles Hendon's lodgings*
18 Solo: 'Miles Hendon's story' (Miles)

*Scene 9: Stateroom at Westminster*
19 Instrumental: Fanfare
20 Trio: 'The royal lesson' (Tom, Humphrey, Snodgrass)

*Scene 10: Miles Hendon's lodgings*

*Scene 11: In the woods, outside London*
21 Duet: 'Edith's story' (Edith, Miles)

*Scene 12: Stateroom at Westminster*
22 Instrumental: 'Make way for the Prince' (Reprise)
23 Chorus: 'The trial' (Hertford, Executioner, Prisoners, Fool, Catherine, Elizabeth, Jane, Tom)

*Scene 13: A London street*

*Scene 14: The stocks*

*Scene 15: The coronation*
24 Instrumental: 'Make way for Edward, Prince of Wales' (Reprise)
25 Chorus: 'Long live the king!' (Full company)

## CAST OF CHARACTERS

**Principal singing roles**
Edward Tudor, Prince of Wales } can be played by one person
Tom Canty, a pauper }
Catherine Parr, the Queen
Lady Jane Grey
Princess Elizabeth Tudor
Miles Hendon, a soldier of fortune
Earl of Hertford, Lord Protector and Edward's uncle

**Smaller singing roles**
John Canty, Tom's father
Mrs Canty, Tom's mother
Henry VIII
Fool
Humphrey Marlow, a whipping boy
Master Snodgrass, a tutor
Edith, a lady of misfortune
Executioner
Prisoner 1
Prisoner 2
Chorus of courtiers, citizens and beggars

**Speaking roles**
Storyteller
Gran Canty
Bet } Tom's sisters
Nan }
Father Andrew, a monk
Palace Guard
Meg, Miles Hendon's housekeeper
Richard, a trickster
A Fop
Archbishop
Sentry

The action covers a period early in the 16th century, immediately preceding the Coronation of King Edward VI. The scenes are set in the Palace of Westminster; in Offal Court in the City of London; and in the streets of London and the surrounding countryside.

## PROPERTIES

*Scene 1*
Material for hawkers and travelling players, etc.
Knife for John.
Begging bowl for Tom.
Halberd for Guard.
*Scene 2*
Table and bench or chair. Curtain. Bed.
Cap for Tom.
*Scene 3*
Flagon, knife, belt, bowl.
Rough table and bench. Bed.
Cudgel for Gran.
Things to wrap in cloth for going away.
*Scene 4*
Nightgown for Tom.
*Scene 5*
Scroll for proclamation.
*Scene 6*
Banquet robes.
Red carpet.
*Scene 7*
Cudgel for John.
Sword for Miles.
Scroll for proclamation.
*Scene 8*
Table and bench. Lute for Miles.
Bed. Cape for Miles.
*Scene 9*
Throne. Chair.
*Scene 10*
Bundle of material for Edward's clothes.
Curtains round bed.
Table and chair.
*Scene 12*
Throne. Axe. Irons and chains.
*Scene 13*
Sack with cat. Cloak for Fop.
*Scene 14*
Stocks. Pillory. Things to throw. Sword and buckler.
*Scene 15*
Throne, crown on cushion. Robe, orb, sceptre, coronets.

ACT 1 SCENE **1** THE DIE IS CAST

*(Cast enters sporadically as individuals, and in pairs and groups. Some erect and adjust the setting. Some entertain with magic/tumbling/juggling/music/dancing/sword swallowing. Some have trays of sweetmeats. All mingle with audience.*

*Last to appear are the* **Musicians**. *Without ceremony, they strike up* 'The Earl of Oxford's march' *and this is the cast's cue to take the stage formally.*

*By the beginning of the second time through of the theme, each member of cast has taken a partner. They dance sedately and, as the theme continues, form a stylised tableau at the end)*

**1 Instrumental: *'The Earl of Oxford's march'***

*(The* **Storyteller** *steps forward)*

**Storyteller:** This evening you will hear a tale that has
Been handed down by fathers to their sons
For fifty and four hundred years and more.
It may be true, it may be only legend
But common sense declares it could have happened

*(General shift of positions, with rhythmic percussion, ending with poor characters one side, rich the other)*

I want you to imagine, if you will,
An England so divided by the law
That only landed gentry and the like
Knew anything of comfort and content.
The rest, like teeming ants upon a hill,
Knew nothing but the struggle to survive.
Between the rich and poor was drawn a line
That separated poverty from plenty.

**2 Chorus: *'The ballad of poverty and plenty'*** (Full company)

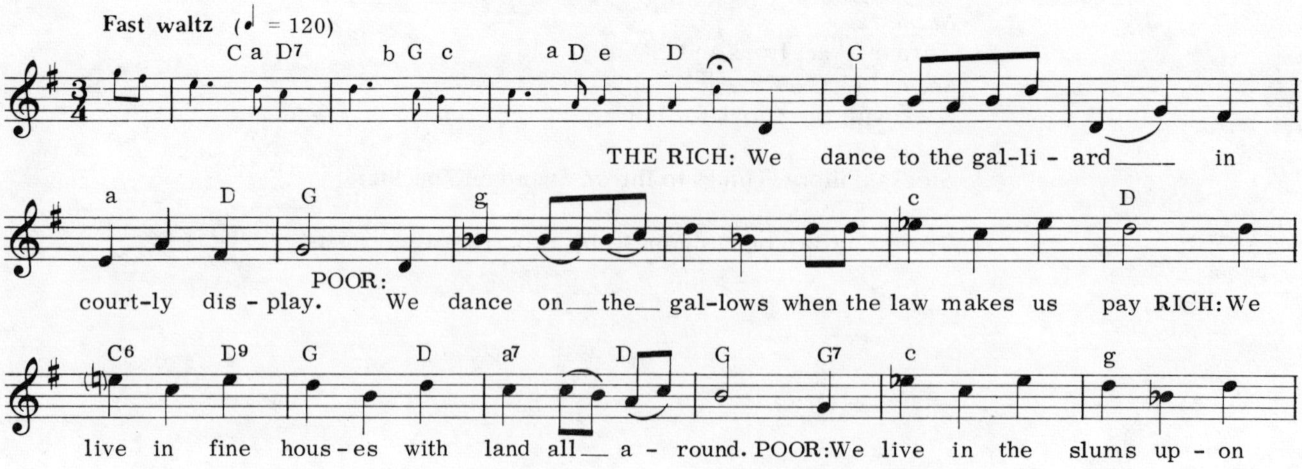

A♭ G C D7 b7 e
what can be found.
(The rich dance while the poor try to beg from them)
a7 D G G7 C+7 D7
b7 e A7 D
POOR: You
We
RICH: Fa-la-la-la - la Fa-la-la-la - la Fa-la- la-la -
C+7 D7 b7 e C
POOR: stink You prink Re - lax your
ache We break our backs to keep
1 la la la
2 la la - la la!
D9 G D9 G
lives a - way. We you at play.
D7 G a D G
RICH: We make mer-ry and we live on the fat of the land. POOR: We
g c D a7 D9 G D
eke out a liv-ing on work done by hand. RICH: Our life is a roun-de-lay of
a7 D G c g A♭ G
rev - el-ry and sport. (P) Our life is a night-mare, our dreams come to naught. We
RICH: Fa-la-la-la - la Fa-la-la-la - la Fa-la-la-la -
C+7 b7 e a7
scrimp, We limp In im - por -

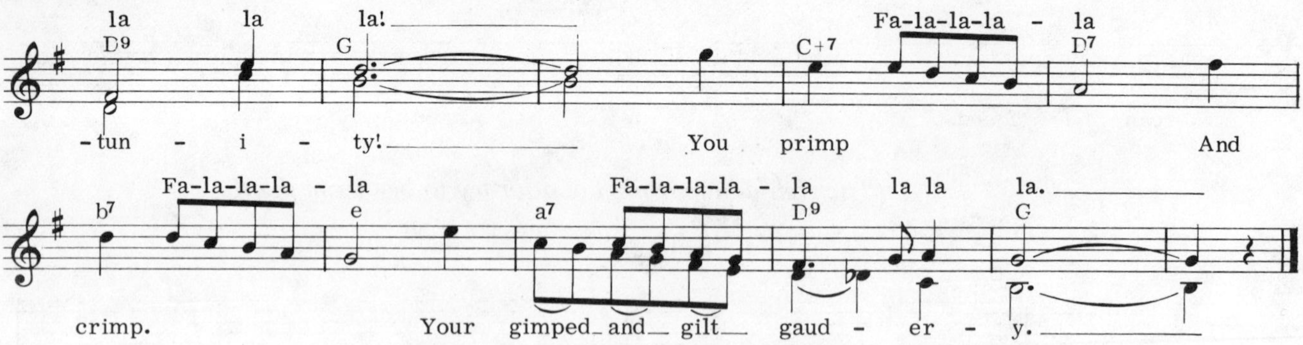


**Storyteller:** Such was the state of England when
Two boys were born in 1537:
The first was Edward Tudor, Prince of Wales,
The son of Bluff King Hal, Henry the Eighth.
All England raised a cheer when *he* was born.

**All:** *(Very abruptly)* Hooray!

**Storyteller:** The other boy born in that self same year
Was Thomas Canty, only son of John
A villain from the slums of Offal Court
Off Pudding Lane, not far from London Bridge.
And nobody rejoiced when *he* was born.

**All:** *(Trailing off grumpily)* Rhubarb . . . rhubarb . . .

*(**John** leads in **Tom** by the ear)*

**John:** Where you been, you little tike?

**Tom:** Out begging, Dad. Like you said.

**John:** What you get? *(Sees)* Call that a day's work? Go beg some more, or I'll break your head.

**Tom:** But people are so poor, Dad. They haven't got any more to spare than we have.

**John:** You'll just have to look more pathetic then, won't you? Like this. *(Feigns wretchedness)* What you got to be so proud of, anyway?

**Tom:** *(Looking at **John**)* Nothing, Father. *(**John** catches sarcasm)*

**John:** *(Producing knife)* Maybe if you was disabled or maimed you'd do better. Would that help? Eh?

*(Enter **Mrs Canty**, **Bet**, **Nan**, **Gran** and **Father Andrew**)*

**Mrs C:** Leave the boy alone, John. He does his best.

**John:** Well, it ain't enough.

**Gran:** He wants a good whippin'.

**Girls:** Gran!

**John:** You're right there, Ma. *(To **Tom**)* Now get begging.

**Mrs C:** But Father Andrew is here to teach Tom and the girls.

**John:** I'll teach him. *(Handles **Tom** roughly)*

**Gran:** It's all this learnin' what's holdin' him back, ask me.

**Bet:** He's the cleverest boy in Offal Court.

**Nan:** Everyone says so.

**Mrs C:** And it's all thanks to Father Andrew.

*(**John** turns on **Father Andrew**, brandishing knife)*

**John:** Well, I'll thank him to leave the boy alone.

**Andrew:** I'll come back later, Mrs Canty. *(Backs off and exits)*

**John:** *(Calling after him)* Not if I'm here, you won't.

**Gran:** Fillin' his head with fancy tales of princes and kings.

**John:** *(Inspired)* That's it, Ma. Outside the palace. *(To **Tom**)* That's where the rich pickings are, lad. Off you go, then.

**Bet:** But he'll be arrested.

**Nan:** He'll be punished.

**John:** He'll be for it if he don't do what I say. Now!

*(**John** offers begging bowl to **Tom**, who takes it reluctantly. He sings and begs to rich passers-by as the poor look on)*

**3 Solo: *'Don't turn me away'*** (Tom)

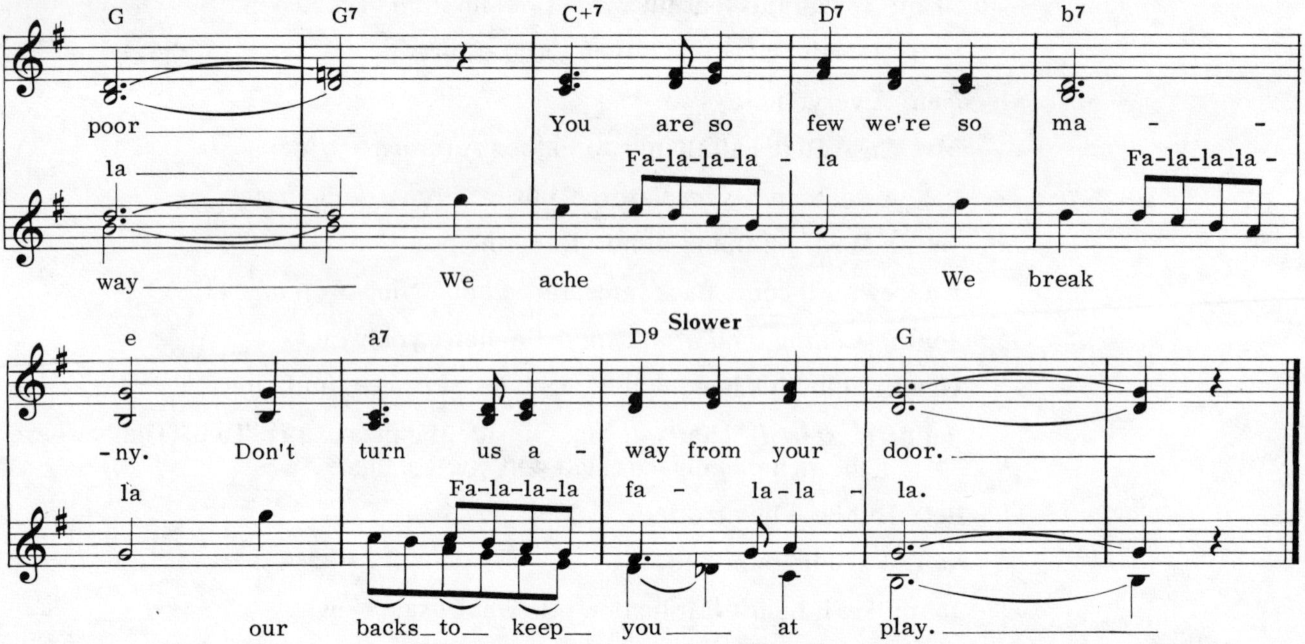


*(The rich disappear, leaving the poor to see* **Tom** *challenged by the* **Guard***)*

**Guard:** Who goes there?

**Tom:** No one. *(Crowd titters)*

**Guard:** What d'you mean, no one? You was begging, wasn't you?

**Tom:** No, sir. *(***Guard** *grabs bowl)*

**Guard:** What's this, then? A flaming plant pot? *(Titters)*

**Tom:** I found it.

**Guard:** G'wan! Get out of it before I fetch you one with me halberd.

**Tom:** I only wanted to catch a glimpse of the prince.

**Guard:** You'll catch the end o' me boot if you don't hop it.

**Tom:** Just one look, please.

**Guard:** *(Grabbing* **Tom***)* All right, you asked for it. *(Crowd reacts)*

**Tom:** Let me go. Where are you taking me?

**Guard:** To the guard house. I'll teach you to beg outside the palace. *(***Tom** *bites his hand)* Agh! You little bleeder! Get in there!

*(He hurls* **Tom** *through upstage exit, and rolls up his sleeves)*

**Crowd:** *(Variously)* Leave him alone. He's only a boy. He never meant no harm. Pick on someone your own size.

*(They form a scrum around the* **Guard***, whose hand we see repeatedly brought down on the unseen* **Tom***. Eventually the* **Guard** *turns on the* **Crowd** *and threatens them)*

**Guard:** You want some too?

*(They back off fearfully and linger at far side of stage.* **Guard** *returns to* **Tom***)*

**Guard:** Now then, m'lad.

*(As he goes to lay into* **Tom**, **Edward** *appears. Crowd gasps)*

**Edward:** Stop!

**Guard:** *(Coming to attention)* Your royal highness!

**Crowd:** *(Variously)* The Prince! The Prince of Wales! His royal highness!

*(***Edward** *crosses and looks down at* **Tom** *offstage)*

**Edward:** Is this the way you treat my father's loyal subjects?

**Guard:** *(Stiffly)* Beg pardon, your highness. He was beggin' at the palace gate. *(Gives bowl to* **Edward***)*

**Edward:** That shows he knows where the money is in this land.

**Crowd:** *(Variously)* Well said, Prince Edward! What a noble prince! Aye!

*(***Edward** *raises a hand to silence them)*

**Edward:** *(To* **Guard***)* You will take him inside. *(Crowd gasps)* You will bathe his wounds. Then you will escort him personally to my cabinet. Is that understood?

**Guard:** At once, your highness. *(He goes)*

**4 Solo and Chorus: *'If I could see'*** (Edward, Tom, Beggar, Rich and Poor)

D9 G D9 G
lives a - way. We you at play.
roy - al realm. Per - o - ver the helm
hard on the poor. way from your door.
Fa la la la la Fa la la la la
D♭+7 E♭7 c7 f7
You stink You prink Re -
If I could see the po - ver - ty a -
Won't someone spare me a pen - ny?
Fa-la-la-la - la la - la Fa la la la la
B♭7 E♭7 A♭ A♭7 D♭+7 E♭7
-lax your lives a - way. We ache We
round this roy - al realm. Per - haps I could per -
Life is so hard for the poor. You are so few we're so

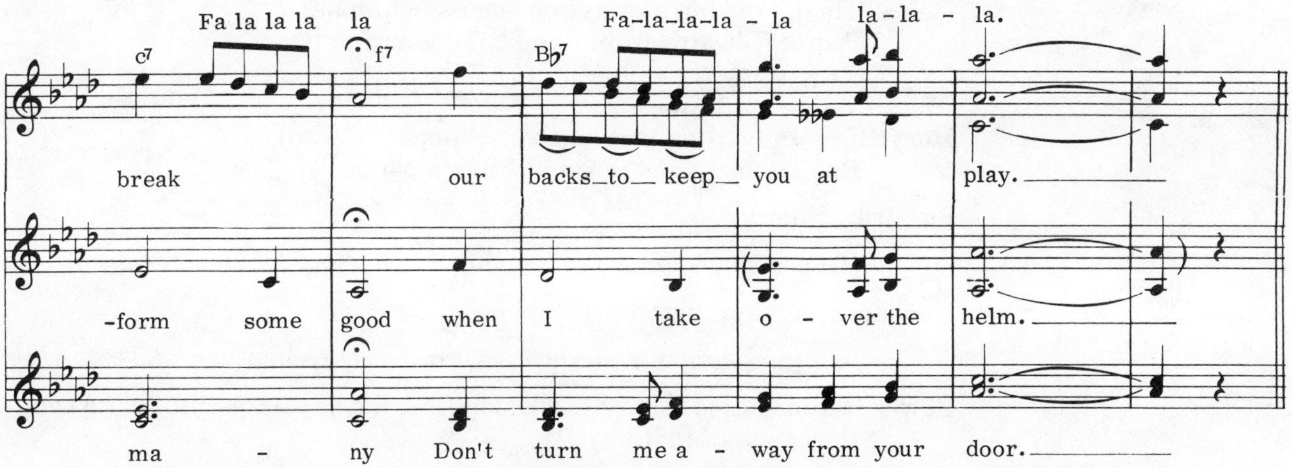


*(**Edward** repeats his chorus and another boy sings Tom's tune as the rich return and the poor resume their taunts)*

*(The rich exit. Then **Edward**)*

**Crowd:** Long live the Prince of Wales! Hooray!

*(The **Guard** returns and thrusts his halberd at them)*

**Guard:** G'wan!

*(The Crowd shrinks back into the shadows. **Guard** exits. We see **Edward** join **Tom** in silhouette. They perform appropriate actions to match the commentary)*

**Storyteller:** What happened in the Prince's room that day
Has now passed into oft-repeated legend.
Be seated, said the Prince. So Tom sat down.
What is your name? Where do you live? And how?
What is it really like to be a pauper?
Tom answered these and other searching questions.
The Prince was deeply moved by what he heard.
For his part, Tom was far too struck with awe
To venture any questions of his own
But even so he could not stop himself
From voicing one thought that lay in his heart:
If I could only wear such clothes as yours,
If only for a moment, I should be
The happiest pauper boy there ever was.
And so you shall, said Edward regally,
And straightaway took off his royal raiments,
And giving them to Tom, said, Give me yours,
For I, too, am intrigued by what *you* wear.
And so the two changed places there and then.
And this is where the story really starts.
For when they stood together at the mirror
It was as if no change had taken place.
There stood a noble prince beside a pauper
And no one would have guessed that they had switched.

Then, noticing a bruise on Tom's right hand,
Prince Edward swore to take the guard to task.

**Edward:** *(Entering and saying angrily)* Guard!

**Storyteller:** Forgetting that he was no longer Edward,
But Thomas Canty, son of John, a pauper!

**Edward:** Guard!

*(**Guard** enters and comes to attention without looking at Edward)*

**Guard:** Your royal highness!

*(Crowd emerges from shadows, muttering recognition of **Tom**)*

**Edward:** I come to tell you I intend to have you punished for your treatment of that boy.

*(**Edward** moves downstage. Crowd titters. **Guard** sees **'Tom'**)*

**Guard:** You! Thrown you out, has he? Well, I'll do for you this time.

*(He lunges and swipes at **Edward** with his halberd, exhorted by crowd)*

**Edward:** *(During lull)* Can you not see I am the Prince of Wales? If you lay one coarse hand on me, you'll hang.

**Guard:** *(Mock salute)* I salute your gracious highness. Now 'op it.

*(And he hurls **Edward** to the cheering crowd, who raise him shoulder-high, crown him with bowl and carry him off)*

**Crowd:** *(Chanting)* Way for his royal highness! Way for the Prince of Wales!

**5 Instrumental: *'The Earl of Oxford's march'*** (Reprise)

*(The pit musicians take up the march which continues under the action)*

**Edward:** Put me down, you fools! I am the Prince of Wales! There's been a terrible mistake. *(As they carry him off)* Thomas!

*(Two or three members of crowd remain or return to remonstrate with **Guard**)*

**Crowd:** *(Variously)* Can't you see he's crazy? He's quite mad. He's nuts. No two ways about it.

**Guard:** *(Menacing them)* Gertcher!

*(They go)*

**Storyteller:** And so the die was cast. The Prince of Wales
Became Tom Canty – for what that was worth.
Leaving the real Tom waiting at the palace,
A pauper in a prince's clothes. And he
Was going to have to wait for quite some time.

*(He bows and exits as the music ends)*

# ACT 1 SCENE 2 THE PRINCE IS MAD

*(A bewildered* **Tom** *peeps out and looks around)*

**Tom:** Your royal highness? Prince Edward? Where can he have gone? This is terrible. I must get these clothes off. *(Takes off cap)* But I have nothing else to wear! The Prince has my clothes. They'll hang me for this. *(Thinks)* I'll hide. *(Looks, stops)* They'll find me for sure. I'll go home. *(Starts, stops)* Dressed like this? *(Thinks)* I'll brazen it out, then. *(Haughty)* Knowest thou not I am the Prince of Wales? Cometh uppeth to the palathe and see me some time. No, no. It might impress the kids in Offal Court, but not here. They'll spot me just like that. And they'll chop my head off just like that. I know they will. I've heard that's how they do things around here. Why, any moment the king himself could come in here . . .

*(During the above,* **Lady Jane Grey** *has entered, unseen by* **Tom***)*

**Jane:** Good morning, my lord.

*(***Tom** *turns and cries in alarm. He falls at her feet)*

**Jane:** God save your royal highness. A kiss would have sufficed.

**Tom:** Be merciful, good lady. I am no one's royal highness. Nor would I presume to know such a fine young woman as yourself.

**Jane:** Not know your loving cousin, the Lady Jane Grey? Edward, is this another of your jokes?

**Tom:** It's no joke, I swear. My name is Tom Canty. I come from Offal Court in the City. And the Prince has gone off with my clothes.

**Jane:** Enough of this, my playful prince. It's time for your lessons.

**Tom:** But it's true, I tell you. I am not the Prince. I am a beggar. Listen. *(Sings, crazily)* Won't someone spare me a penny? Life is so hard for the poor. You are so few, we're so many. Don't turn me away from your door . . . *(etc)*

**Jane:** *(Overlapping)* Lord save us, the Prince has gone mad! *(She runs to the door)* Lord Hertford! Elizabeth! The Prince is mad!

*(She takes another anguished look at* **Tom** *and rushes out, leaving him incanting his beggar's song. Her parting words are echoed by voices offstage, receding to distance)*

**Voices:** The Prince is mad! The Prince is mad! The Prince is mad!

*(***Jane** *returns with* **Hertford**, **Catherine** *and* **Elizabeth** *as song intro plays. The court* **Fool** *follows them in and takes position by the door.* **Lord Hertford** *approaches* **Tom** *tentatively)*

**6 Chorus: *'The Prince is mad!'*** (Hertford, Tom, Jane, Catherine, Fool, Henry, Elizabeth)

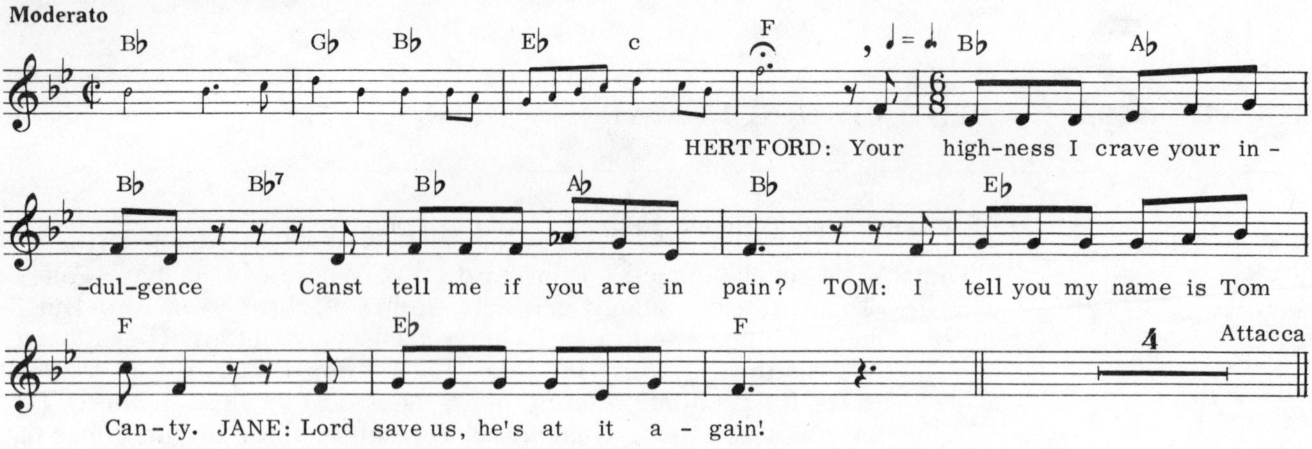


**Hertford:** How long has he been in this humour?

**Jane:** I don't know. I found him a minute ago. *(***Fool** *steps forward)*

**Fool:** Shall I tell him a funny story?

**Elizabeth:** No.

**Hertford:** We must get through to him. *(They return to* **Tom***)*

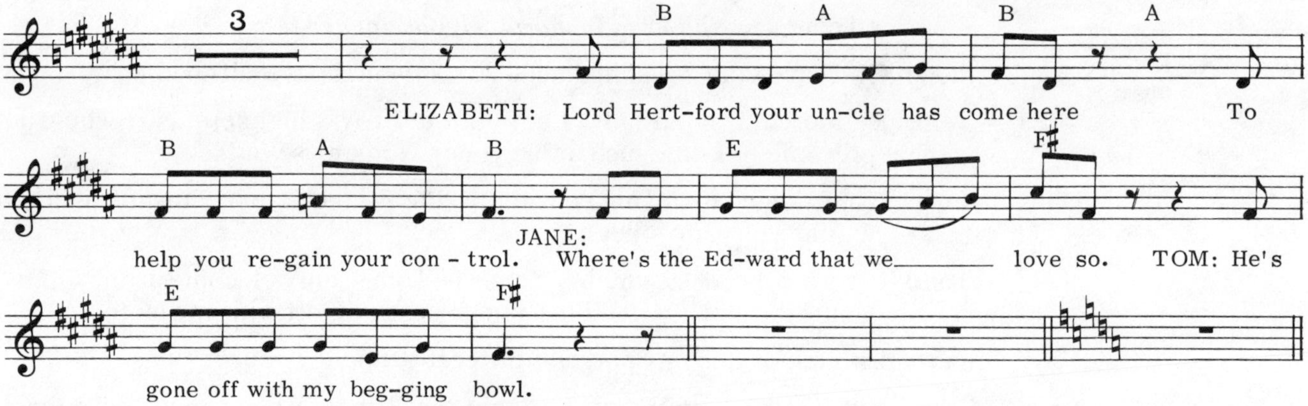


*(Music over dialogue)*

**Hertford** What is he talking about?

**Elizabeth:** I've no idea.

**Jane:** *(To Elizabeth)* Try again, your highness. *(They return to* **Tom***)*

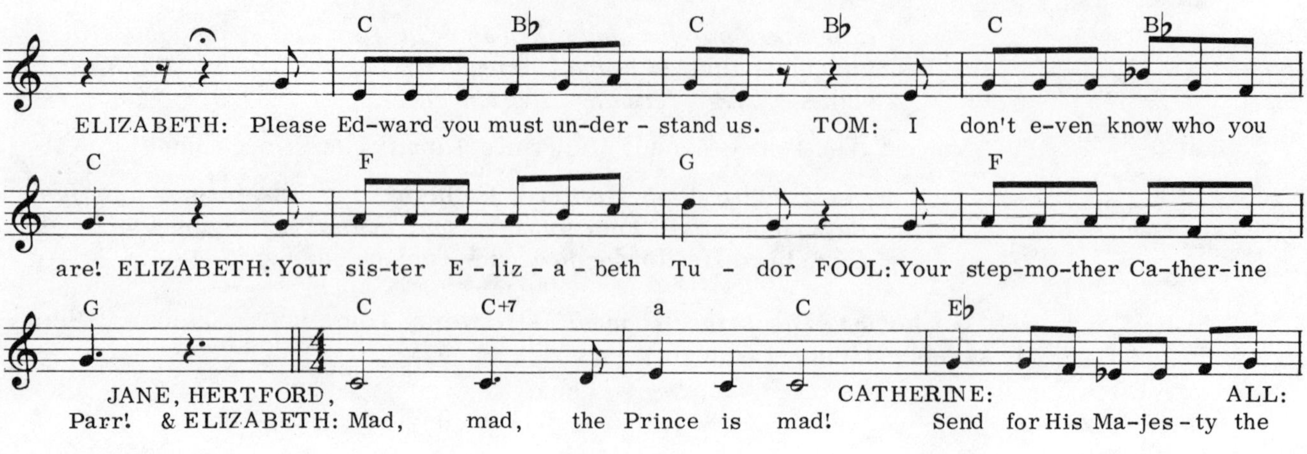

**Catherine:** What is your opinion, Lord Hertford?

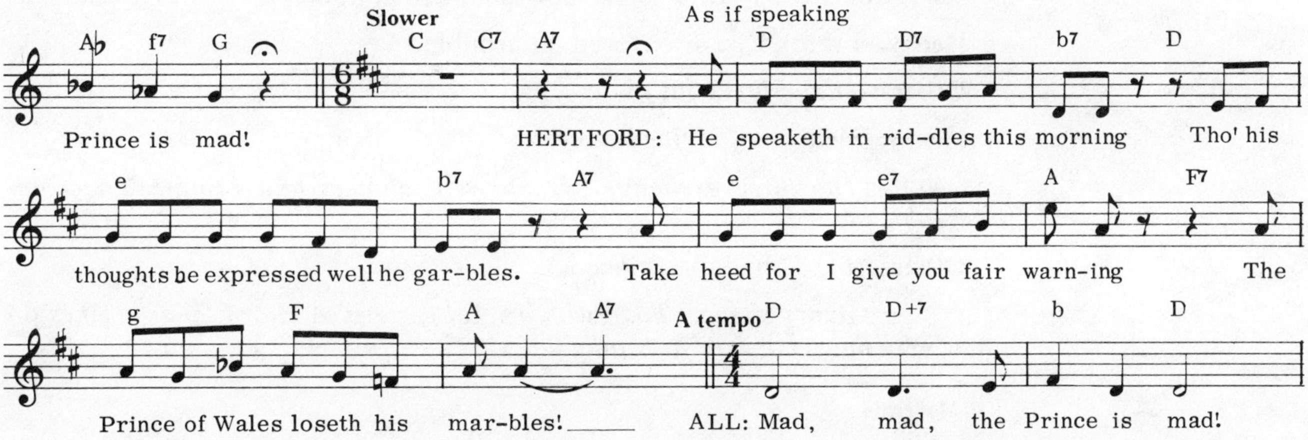


*(Chord as* **Henry** *enters with* **Fool** *and bluffly approaches* **Tom***)*

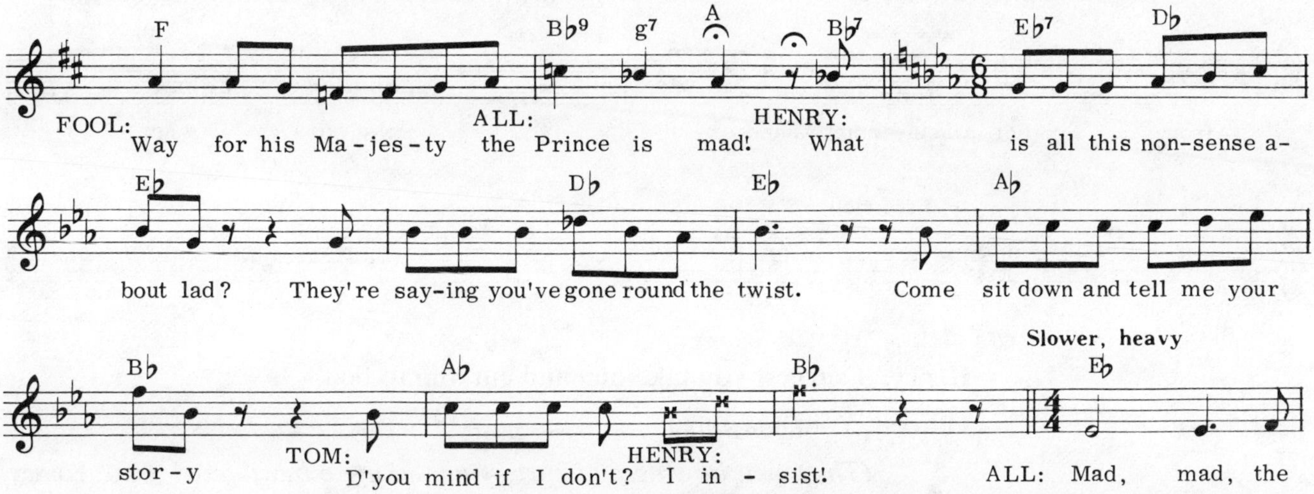


*(He takes* **Tom** *to table and sits with him)*

*(**Henry** remains talking quietly to **Tom**. **Hertford** and **Girls** strain to overhear. The **Fool** remains stationed at door)*

**Henry:** I think I've discovered the trouble.

**Others:** *(Eagerly)* Your majesty?

**Henry:** He's stark raving bonkers.

*(The three exchange 'we knew it' glances and resume, unaccompanied)*

**Others:** Mad, mad the Prince is . . .

*(**Henry** silences them with a regal gesture. A chord, and he takes up the verse with slow poignancy)*

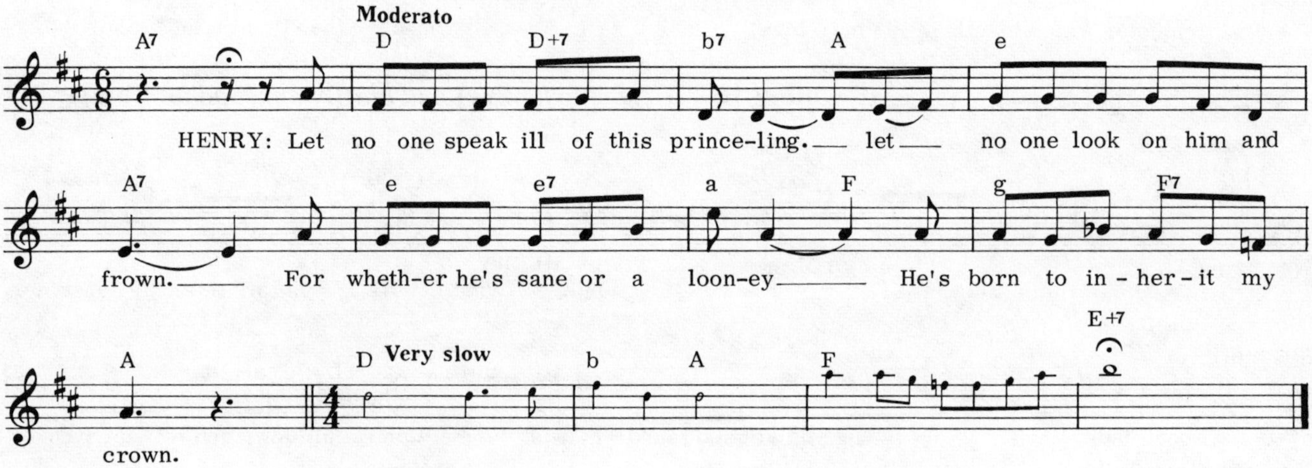


**Henry:** I suggest you take him and put him to bed.

**Others:** Your majesty.

*(They exit, bowing and curtseying, taking a bewildered **Tom**. **Henry** goes to table and sits, deep in thought)*

**Henry:** Fool?

**Fool:** *(Stepping forward)* Your majesty?

**Henry:** Is it possible to kill with kindness?

**Fool:** So they say, your majesty.

**Henry:** *(Ruefully)* Then that boy's life has never been in danger from me.

**7 Solo:** ***'Have I been too hard on the boy?'*** (Henry)

*(The **Fool** sits and strums his lute as **Henry** sings. As **Henry** loses himself in thought we see **Tom** being put to bed)*

*(**Henry** exits, taking **Tom**'s discarded hat with him. The **Fool** bows as **Henry** exits. He moves the table to 'poor' side of stage, then exits with two chairs)*

ACT 1 SCENE **3**

# THE PRINCE'S TROUBLES BEGIN

*(**John Canty** hurls **Edward** onto stage before him)*

**John:** Get in there, you little bleeder! *(Takes off belt)* I'll teach you to play games with me.

*(Enter **Mrs C**, **Bet** and **Nan**, and **Gran** with a flagon from which she swigs)*

**Mrs C:** John! What's happening? *(Sees **Edward**)* Tom!

*(**Mrs C** and **Nan** help **Edward** up. **Gran** merely swigs)*

**Gran:** What's he done now? I'll crown him.

**John:** Oh, he'd love that, he would. Being crowned. *(Takes swig)*

**Mrs C:** How do you mean?

**John:** I found him down by the palace. Playing at princes and kings again. With all the rabble. Shoulder-high they was carryin' him.

**Gran:** How much did he get?

**John:** *(Showing bowl)* Not a groat. Look at that. After all the trainin' I've given him, too.

**Gran:** He's a disgrace to the family name, he is. *(Takes swig)*

**John:** That's not the 'alf of it, neither. This royal business is going to his head. Guess what he said when I collared him.

**Gran:** No. Go on.

**John:** *(Mock haughty)* Unhand me, you cur, for I am the Prince of Wales.

**Gran:** He never did!

**John:** He did.

**Edward:** I *am* the Prince of Wales.

**Mrs C:** Tom!

**John:** There you are.

**Edward:** *(To **Mrs C**)* Your son is at the palace in my place.

**Mrs C:** *(Broken)* Oh, Tom.

**Bet:** *(Comforting her)* Don't upset yourself, Mum.

**Nan:** *(To **John**)* You've done this to him!

**John:** *(Raising fist)* G'wan! Or I'll do for you an' all.

**Mrs C:** He's your son! Don't you feel anything for him?

**John:** Yeah! Contempt! He's useless. Fact I wonder sometimes if he's my son at all.

**Mrs C:** That's a horrible thing to say.

**John:** Well . . .

**8 Duet: *'No boy of mine'*** (John, Mrs Canty)

**Mrs C:** Leave him alone. He's had enough.

**John:** Well, so have I. The ungrateful brat.

**Mrs C:** What have you ever done to earn his gratitude? You don't even understand him.

**John:** What d'you mean?

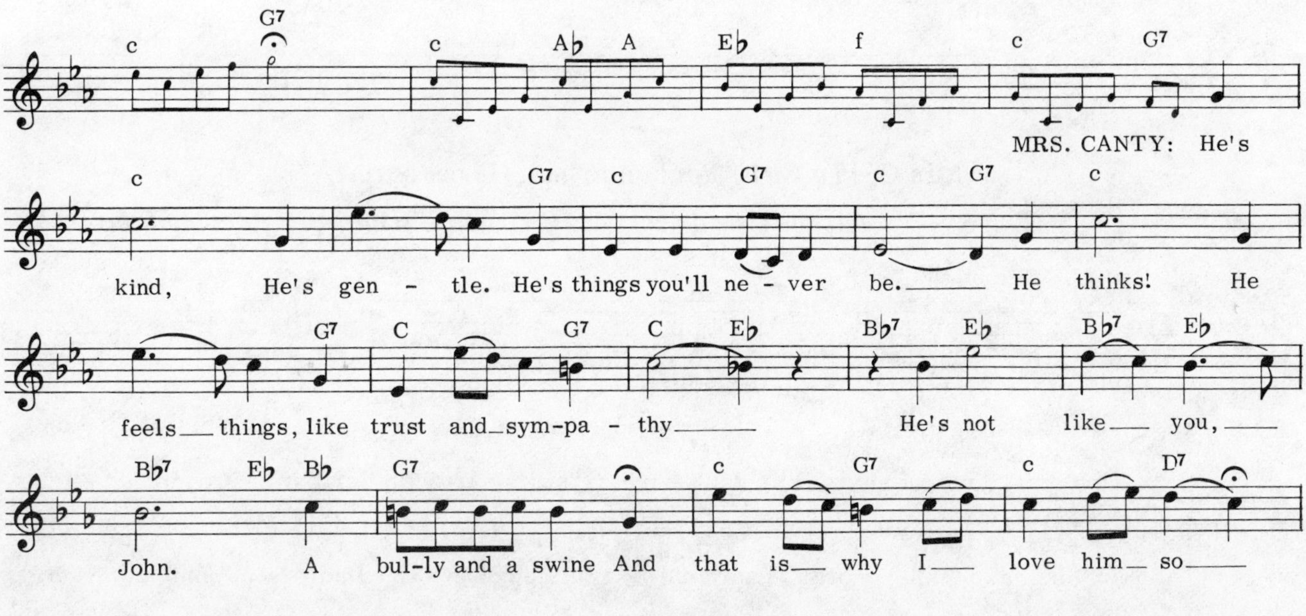

**John:** No wonder he's soft. The way you've protected him.

**Mrs C:** With you around, he's needed it.

**John:** Well, someone's got to take a firm hand with him.

**Mrs C:** Why?

**John:** So's he can hold his head up in the world. That's why.

**Mrs C:** *(To* **Girls***)* Put him to bed. He needs rest.

*(As the girls do so,* **Mrs C** *restrains* **John** *from grabbing him)*

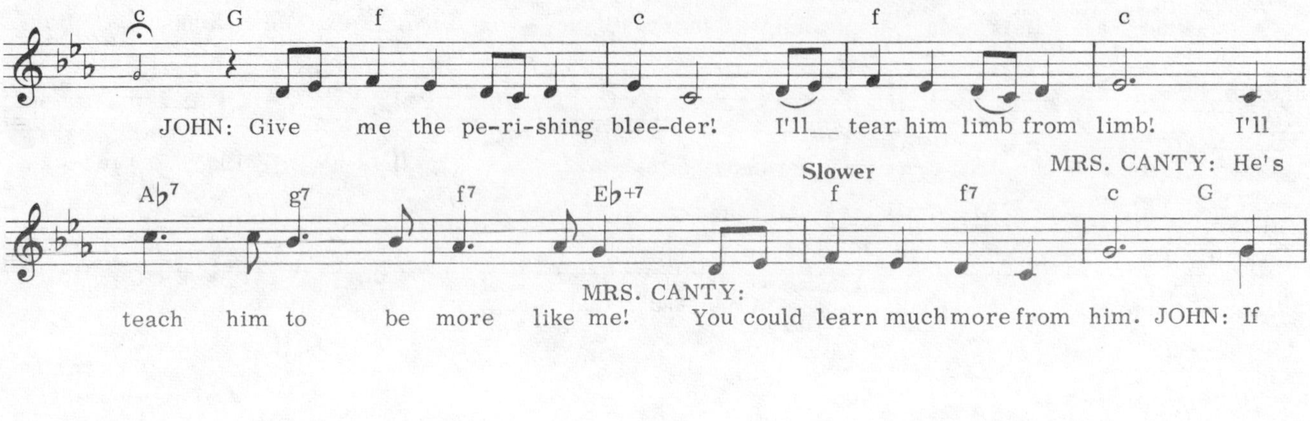

**John:** Give us another pull on that flagon, ma.

**Gran:** It's empty, son.

**John:** Damn and blast it! Well, I'm not going short tonight. I'm off to get some more.

**Gran:** And how are you going to pay for it?

**John:** *(Showing knife)* I'm sure someone'll treat me.

**Gran:** I'll come with you. Case you needs 'elp.

*(She pulls a cudgel out of her skirts and follows* **John** *out.* **Mrs C** *looks at where girls are putting* **'Tom'** *to bed and breaks down)*

*(***Nan** *and* **Bet** *comfort* **Mrs Canty**. *There is a knock at the door)*

**Mrs C:** Come in. *(***Father Andrew** *enters)* Father Andrew!

**Andrew:** I came as soon as I heard.

**Bet:** You heard?

**Andrew:** About Thomas' escapade at the palace, yes.

**Nan:** How?

**Andrew:** The talk is of nothing else. How is he?

**Mrs C:** *Who* is he would be more to the point.

**Andrew:** I don't understand.

**Bet:** Nor do we.

**Nan:** He thinks he's the Prince of Wales.

**Andrew:** The Prince of Wales? That's absurd.

**Mrs C:** Absurd or not, that's what he believes.

**Andrew:** Clearly his meeting with the Prince has turned his head.

**Bet:** He met the Prince?

**Nan:** He met the Prince of Wales?

**Andrew:** Yes. Did he not tell you? The palace guard was about to whip him for begging when the prince came out and took him in.

**Mrs C:** What, into the palace?

**Girls:** No!

**Andrew:** Yes. He was in there some time, by all accounts. Till the guard got hold of him again and threw him out on his ear.

**Mrs C:** Perhaps that's what has numbed his brain.

**Andrew:** Where is he now?

**Bet:** We put him to bed.

**Andrew:** Is he asleep?

**Nan:** He wasn't just now.

**Andrew:** Perhaps I could have a word with him?

**Mrs C:** I wish you would, Father.

*(We hear* **John** *and* **Gran** *returning, singing)*

**Bet:** It's Dad.

**Mrs C:** *(To* **Andrew***)* Go in quickly, before he sees you.

*(***John** *enters, followed by* **Gran***)*

**Nan:** Too late.

**John:** I warned you, holy man.

**Mrs C:** John, please.

**Andrew:** I heard about Tom. I thought I might help.

**John:** You've done enough, mate.

**Gran:** We'll give him all the help he needs.

**John:** *(Approaching bedroom)* That's right.

**Mrs C:** What are you going to do?

**John:** *(Taking off his belt)* I'm gonna belt the lights out of him. That's what I'm gonna do.

**Andrew:** Not while I'm here, you're not.

**John:** Oh? Fighting words from a man of the cloth?

**Gran:** What you gonna do, then? Put one on him?

**Andrew:** I won't fight. But I'll keep him from beating his son if I can.

**John:** Out of my way . . . *(Sneering)* . . . Father!

*(He pushes past* **Andrew** *and exits to where* **'Tom'** *is.* **Father Andrew** *follows. We see their silhouettes)*

**Andrew:** *(Off)* Mr Canty! I cannot stand by and allow you to . . .

**John:** *(Off)* Well, take that, then, you meddling swine!

*(All gasp as* **Andrew** *falls to the floor)*

**Mrs C:** John, no!

**Gran:** What's he done? The fool! The fool!

*(***John** *emerges with red-stained knife. He looks shaken)*

**John:** Well, he stopped me from beating our Tom all right.

**Nan:** Dad! How could you? *(***Nan** *and* **Bet** *exit.* **Bet** *returns)*

**Bet:** He's dead! *(She exits again)*

**Gran:** You've done it now!

**Mrs C:** John!

**Gran:** Why couldn't you have waited?

**Mrs C:** A man of the cloth!

**Gran:** Got him in some quiet spot?

**Mrs C:** Everyone will know it was you.

**Gran:** You could have done for him and got clean away.

**John:** Shut up! *(Wipes knife and puts it away)* We'll have to get out of here. Bet! Nan! Get Tom up and dressed.

*(The girls peer out at* **John***)*

**Mrs C:** What, now?

**John:** Yes. Now. *(He begins wrapping things in cloth)*

**Mrs C:** But why?

**John:** Do you know what the punishment is for what I just done? They'll hang, draw and quarter me.

**Gran:** They will an' all. Hangs you up by the neck, they does. Slow, like. An' before you has time to strangle they slits open yer gizzard, takes out yer heart an' shows it to you, still beating. Then if you're lucky you dies before they cuts you up into four quarters just like a pig. I know. I seen it done.

**John:** *(Sickened)* Come on, ma. Come on, you lot. Let's go.

*(***John***,* **Mrs C***,* **Gran***, the* **Girls** *and* **Edward** *all exit)*

**9 Instrumental:** ***'No boy of mine' / 'The Prince is mad!'*** (Reprise)

*(***Fool** *enters, places table and sits cross-legged, asleep)*

## ACT 1 SCENE 4 IN WESTMINSTER PALACE

*(***Tom** *appears from prince's bedroom in nightgown, yawning.* **Fool** *rises at once and bows)*

**Fool:** Good morrow, your highness. I trust you slept well.

**Tom:** No, I didn't. I dreamed I had taken the place of the Prince of Wales. And when I woke up, I had.

**Fool:** Oh dear. *(Aside)* He was funny at dinner last night, too.

**Tom:** Who are you?

**Fool:** Will Somers, the King's Fool, your highness.

**Tom:** Fool? What's that?

**Fool:** I'm supposed to make his majesty laugh. To take his mind off matters of state.

**Tom:** Oh, a jester. I've read about such things.

**Fool:** The King will be pleased that some of your memory is restored, sir.

**Tom:** There's nothing wrong with my memory. It's getting people to take me seriously I have trouble with.

**Fool:** Not like me. When people start taking me serious, I'm out of a job.

**Tom:** What do you think they'll do to me?

**Fool:** Do to you, sir?

**Tom:** When they find out I'm speaking the truth?

**Fool:** Well, let me see. It can't be as bad as being caught in a lie. And that's the truth. No, it's quite the reverse. So I reckon they'll put the rabble in the stocks and let you throw rotten fruit at them. Which reminds me, your highness, do you know what one strawberry said to the other strawberry?

**Tom:** No.

*(***Elizabeth** *and* **Jane** *enter)*

**Eliz:** If we hadn't been found in the same bed, we wouldn't be in this jam.

**Fool:** *(Bowing to girls)* Your highness. Milady.

**Eliz:** *(To* **Edward**, *with a kiss)* Good morning, Edward.

**Jane:** *(Curtseying)* Your highness.

**Eliz:** Are you making my brother laugh, Will?

**Fool:** I live in hopes, your highness.

**Jane:** Do carry on, Will.

**Fool:** That I will. As the king himself always says: If there's anyone who will make people laugh with a will, Will will.

**Eliz:** Go on, then, jester. Do your worst.

**Fool:** All right. Answer me this. What's yellow and stupid?

**Jane:** Don't know.

**Fool:** Thick custard. Which candle burns longer, the wax or the tallow?

**Eliz:** Well, let's see . . .

**Fool:** Neither. They both burn shorter. What did the busy man do when his clock stopped?

**Tom:** *(By now drawn)* I don't know. What did the busy man do when his clock stopped?

**Fool:** Nothing. He didn't have the time. Two men. One tall, the other short. Which is the laziest?

**Jane:** Don't know.

**Fool:** The tall one.

**Eliz:** Why?

**Fool:** He lies longest in bed. What did the would-be suicide say?

**Tom:** I don't know. What did he say?

**Fool:** I'll kill myself if it's the last thing I do.

**Jane:** Tell us the one about the jester.

**Fool:** What, Nestor Chester?

**Jane:** Yes. *(She and* **Eliz** *are laughing in anticipation)*

**Fool:** Invested jester to the Earl of Leicester?

**Eliz:** Yes.

**Fool:** Who pressed his attentions on Leicester's wife Esther?

**E/J:** Yes.

**Fool:** Well, this best of jesters depressed her when he manifested himself as a pestering molester on a desperate quest to divest her breast and wrest her westward to a sequestered nest in Preston. Nevertheless, the prepossessing Esther, blessed with an effervescent zest for a jest, assessed it best to acquiesce to his express request, and progress under duress to the suggested address, lest the jester Nestor's professed excess of suppressed prowess get the best of him. Investigations at Leicester's behest suggest the earliest arrest of the bestial pest in question.

**10 Instrumental:** ***Fanfare***

*(***Hertford*** steps in and takes position)*

**Hertford:** Way for His Majesty the King. *(All bow/curtsey)*

**Henry:** *(Entering)* Never mind all that. Any luck, Will?

**Fool:** A little, your majesty.

**Eliz:** In fact he was laughing just before you arrived, father.

**Henry:** Is that so? *(To* **Tom***)* You find our Will amusing, my son?

**Tom:** Oh yes, indeed, sire, and I only wish the Prince of Wales could have been here to enjoy it, too.

**Henry:** Oh dear.

**Hertford:** Have patience, sire. I fear he needs more time. The physicians say . . .

**Henry:** The physicians say that time is something I do not have in abundance, Lord Hertford. We must do something about this boy now, or England will have a lunatic on the throne.

*(He goes into a coughing fit.* **Elizabeth** *and* **Jane** *go to his aid)*

**Hertford:** *(To* **Fool***)* Send for the Queen at once.

**Fool:** Yes, milord. *(Aside)* You get used to it after a while. *(Goes)*

**Hertford:** I will pursue a gentle line of questioning, with due regard to his condition.

*(He takes* **Tom** *gently aside as song intro plays, then, sternly)*

**11 Chorus: *'Who do you think you are?'*** (Hertford, Tom, Catherine, Jane, Henry, Fool, Elizabeth)

*(After verse 1 the* **Queen** *enters, heralded by the* **Fool***. Music continues over dialogue until verse 2)*

A b e A7
Is that a-ny way to treat a man with gout? I
When all he can do is pla-ti-tu-di-nise In
D D7 e7 A D D7 Slower
think you've gone too far. Who do you think you are? TWO GIRLS:
strange ver-na-cu-lar HENRY: Who do you think you are? There
G+7 C+7 f♯7 B7 e7 A7
must be something we can do to bring him back to earth And to save him from this third de-
D D7 G+7 C+7 f♯7 b7
-gree We've tried a lit-tle mirth to re-mind him of his birth what
E7 A7 B♭7 E♭
more help can there be? ALL: Who do you think you are? In
D♭ G f
deal-ing with your sick-ness we have drained the pharm-o-coe-pi-
c7 E♭ D♭
-a Your ma-la-dy's still un-ex-plained. How can we put a
G E♭
man up-on the throne Who's li-ving with-in a strange world of his
F7 B♭ c7 c7 c7 f
own Un-a-ble to rule the land be-cause he's prone
B♭7 E♭ E♭7 C7 A♭ f7 B♭7
to neu-ras-the-ni-a. Who do you think you
E♭ f7 B♭7 E♭
are? TOM: I've told you a-gain and a-gain!

**Fool:** Her majesty the Queen!

**Cath:** Henry! What happened? Are you all right?

**Henry:** Don't fuss, my dear. It's nothing but a mild attack of apoplexy.

**Hertford:** *(Crossing)* I'm afraid the prince is no better, your majesty.

**Cath:** *(Crossing to* **Tom***)* We'll see about that!

*(At the end of the song, they gather round* **Tom** *solicitously and escort him out. Left alone, the* **Fool** *steps downstage)*

**Fool:** *(Confidentially)* The song is ended, but the malady lingers on.

*(Blackout)*

**12 Instrumental:** ***'No boy of mine'*** (Reprise)

## ACT 1 SCENE 5 A LONDON STREET

*(***John**, **Gran**, **Bet**, **Nan**, **Mrs C** *and* **Edward** *shamble on wearily)*

**Bet:** How much further, Dad?

**John:** Keep yer flamin' voice down!

**Gran:** You'll 'ave the law on us.

**Mrs C:** Young Tom's ready to drop.

**Edward:** I'm not used to walking long distances. Especially barefoot.

**John:** What d'you mean? You're on your feet beggin' all day.

**Gran:** An' you never 'ad a pair of shoes in yer life.

**Nan:** Where are we going anyway?

**John:** Upriver. Hampton Court way. I've heard tell there's boats for the takin' up there. Very quiet it is. We can slip away without anyone noticin'. Oh yes, we'll get a boat all right. No one about up there. Very quiet, it is.

*(His voice trails off as they all exit and* **Storyteller** *enters. He unrolls a Royal Proclamation)*

**Storyteller:** Hear ye! Hear ye! Concerning the Royal Progress by river to Hampton Court. His Majesty the King being indisposed, his place at the pageant will be taken by His Royal Highness the Prince Edward. Be it known that all boats requisitioned for the comfort of his highness' honoured guests shall be accorded freedom of the river, and none but these shall venture on to the water this night. On pain of death. Long live the King!

*(***Storyteller** *exits)*

ACT 1

SCENE **6** TOM ACCEPTS HIS PART

(**Hertford** *enters with suit of fine princely robes)*

**Hertford:** Your highness! Your highness! Your banquet robes are here.

(**Tom** *enters, half dressed)*

**Tom:** I'm not going. It wouldn't be right.

**Hertford:** But your father has commanded it.

**Tom:** He's not my father. He's my King.

**Hertford:** All the more reason, surely, for you to do what pleases him.

**Tom:** My only wish is for his son to be restored.

**Hertford:** A wish we all devoutly share, your highness.

**Tom:** Then why don't you get up a search party?

**Hertford:** *(Aside)* Lord save us!

**Cath:** *(Entering)* Edward! Are you not dressed yet? The carriage is here to take you to the barge.

**Hertford:** He is still sick at heart, your majesty.

**Cath:** Sick or not, he's going to that pageant. Fool!

**Fool:** *(Entering)* Yes, your majesty.

**Cath:** Have the carriage brought round at once.

**Fool:** *(Aside)* Why? Has it fainted? *(Aloud)* Yes, your majesty. *(Goes)*

**Cath:** And remember this, my stepson. You may be sick, but your father the King is sicker.

**Hertford:** Your derangement has caused him much distress.

**Cath:** He has taken to his bed, and will see no one save Archbishop Cranmer. Not even me.

**Hertford:** Has it come to that?

**Cath:** *(Gravely)* It has.

**Tom:** *(Concerned)* God save the King!

**Cath:** But he *has* asked me to entreat you to hide your infirmity until it has passed.

**Hertford:** For his sake, you must deny to no one that you truly are the Prince of Wales . . . *(***Tom** *hesitates)* . . . Your Highness?

**Tom:** I only wish I could help you . . .

**Cath:** Please, Edward. He's so ill.

**Tom:** I understand. I will do all I can to please him.

**Hertford:** Thank heaven.

**Fool:** *(Entering)* The carriage has been revived.

**Cath:** What?

**Fool:** Brought round, your majesty.

**Cath:** Good. Come, Lord Hertford. *(They help* **Tom** *dress as he sings)*

**13 Solo:** ***'I am no prince'*** (Tom)

**14 Instrumental:** ***'Make way for the Prince'***

*(Music fades on scene change with dialogue)*

ACT 1 SCENE **7** MILES HENDON

*(**John** and **family** arrive amidst the activity. **Sentry** is on duty)*

**Gran:** I thought you said it was goin' to be quiet. Very quiet, you said it was goin' to be.

**John:** I can't understand it. It's busier than Smithfield Market.

**Edward:** Of course!

**John:** Eh?

**Edward:** The royal pageant. It's tonight. I'm supposed to be here.

**Gran:** Well, you are here, ain't you? Stupid clod.

**Edward:** They must let me in. *(Runs to **Sentry**)*

**Mrs C:** Tom, no!

**Girls:** Tom, come back!

**Gran:** C'm'ere, you little tike.

**John:** Come back here!

*(But **Edward** is already struggling with **Sentry**)*

**Sentry:** Now then, now then. What's the hurry?

**Edward:** You must let me pass. I am the Prince of Wales.

**Sentry:** Pleased to meet you. I'm the King of France.

**Edward:** My father is in there. I must see him.

**Sentry:** He's not, you know. He's in bed with 'is leg.

**Edward:** Oh no! Is he ill?

**Sentry:** How should I know? All I know is the Prince of Wales is in there takin' his place. Now run along, there's a good boy.

**Edward:** The Prince of Wales? You've seen him?

**Sentry:** Course I have. A million times.

**Edward:** You've seen him tonight?

**Sentry:** Yeah. Real 'andsome, he was. All done out in his best.

**Edward:** How dare he? I'll have him flayed alive. Let me pass.

**Sentry:** Look, I've been nice to you, son. I don't wanna get nasty.

**John:** *(Approaching)* Beg pardon, sir. Is my son annoying you?

**Sentry:** *(Bowing)* I'm sorry, your majesty. I didn't recognise you.

**John:** Forgive him. He's a little touched in the head.

**Edward:** I am not.

**John:** *(Through teeth)* You will be if you don't come quiet. *(Shows cudgel)*

**Edward:** I won't. I won't. They've got to let me in. I *am* the Prince of Wales. Let me go! Let me go!

*(This as* **John** *drags him back to family and onlookers)*

**John:** All right. You asked for it. *(Holds* **Edward**, *raises cudgel)*

**Mrs C:** John, don't be a fool.

**John:** He's the Prince of Wales. I'm gonna crown him. It's only fair.

*(***Miles Hendon** *appears and snatches cudgel from* **John***'s hand)*

**Miles:** I wouldn't call it fair, exactly.

**John:** *(Turning)* And who might you be, friend?

**Miles:** No friend of yours, depend on it. But I'll be an ally to this poor youth.

**John:** He's my son.

**Miles:** And that gives you the right to break his head with clubs?

**John:** I'll break his spirit.

**Mrs C:** If he has any left.

**Man:** He's mad, squire.

**Girl:** He thinks he's the Prince of Wales.

**Man:** He's barmy!

**Gran:** He's off his chump, and that's a fact.

**Mrs C:** He's ill. Can't anyone see that?

**John:** Course I can. And I know just how to cure him. Gimme that cudgel.

**Miles:** *(Doing so)* All right. *(Murmurs from crowd)*

**John:** *(Gloating)* That's better.

**Miles:** Although how you're going to use it with a broken arm is a mystery to me.

**John:** I haven't got a broken arm.

**Miles:** You will have if you raise it against this boy. *(Draws sword)*

**John:** What's he to you, anyway?

**Miles:** A lot more than he is to you, clearly.

**15 Solo:** ***'The high cost of living'*** (Miles)

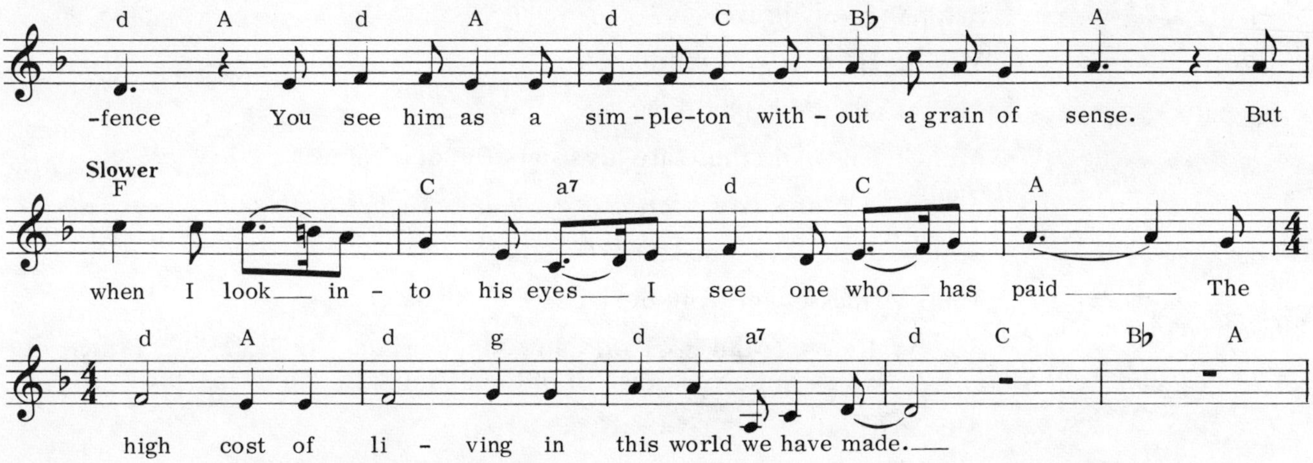


**John:** G'wan! You're as daft as he is!

**Miles:** I'd rather be daft as him than ugly as you!

*(**John** goes for **Miles** with his cudgel, **Miles** fends him off with his sword, and draws **Edward** away from the others)*

**Miles:** *(To **John**)* Now clear out, you villain, or you'll discover the high cost of defying the sword of Miles Hendon.

**John:** All right. You win. But I'll be back. I'll have him.

**Gran:** He will an' all. *(She and **John** exit. Canty **women** cross to **Miles**)*

**Mrs C:** Oh, thank you, sir.

**Nan:** You're very kind.

**Bet:** And very brave.

**Mrs C:** He needs a friend like you.

**Miles:** You are his mother?

**Mrs C:** Yes. And these are his sisters Bet and Nan.

*(A* **Man** *enters bearing a scroll, approaches* **Sentry***)*

**Sentry:** Halt. Who goes there?

**Man:** A messenger from the palace.

**Sentry:** Enter. *(***Man** *goes in)* Now stand aside, you lot. The Prince of Wales will be coming out of the banquet in a minute.

**All:** Hooray!

**16 Chorus: *'Make way for Edward, Prince of Wales'*** (Full company)

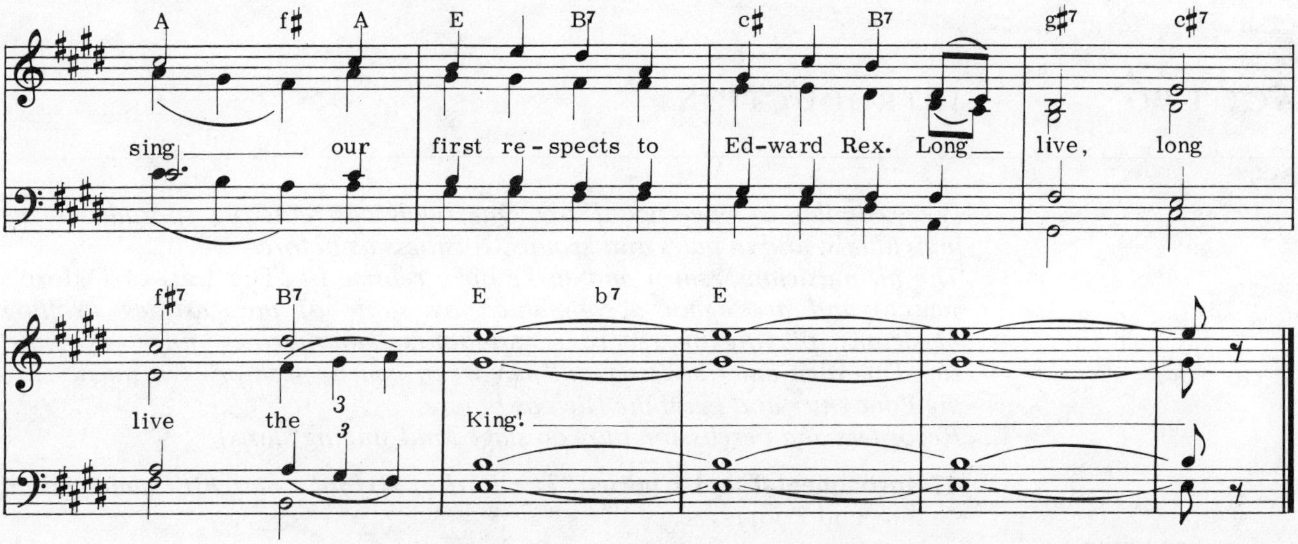


*(Music over dialogue as* **Hertford** *appears, holding scroll. Crowd buzzes in confusion/anticipation.* **Hertford** *reads scroll)*

**Hertford:** It is with deep regret that I have to inform his loyal subjects that the King is dead. Long live the King!

*(***Edward** *collapses.* **Miles** *and* **women** *support him)*

*End of Act One*

## ACT TWO INTRODUCTION

*(Very similar to opening of Act One, with cast entering sporadically as individuals, and in pairs and groups. Business as before.*
*The pit musicians return and strike up a reprise of* 'The Earl of Oxford's march' *and are again accompanied by some of the cast, as strolling musicians, playing on recorders, tambours, tambourines, finger cymbals, etc. The* **Rich** *enter sedately and cavort in courtly fashion. On music cue, the* **Poor** *enter and taunt the Rich as before.*
*Recorders and percussion play on stage until singing starts)*

**17 Instrumental and Chorus: *'The Earl of Oxford's march'/'Falala'*** (Rich and Poor)

*(All exit, going their separate ways)*

ACT 2

SCENE **8** MILES HENDON'S LODGINGS

(**Miles** *leads* **Edward** *into his lodgings.* **Edward** *is weary, near-broken)*

**Miles:** This is where I live. No palace for a prince, I grant you. But it's all I have.

**Edward:** I am the prince no more.

**Miles:** Ha! The light at the end of the tunnel!

**Edward:** I am the king now.

**Miles:** False alarm. You really live this fantasy, don't you?

**Edward:** It's no fantasy. A nightmare, perhaps. *(Collapses at table)*

**Miles:** Forgive me – er – your majesty. My etiquette is rusty. *(Aside)* I considered life had been cruel to me. I see now how lightly it has treated me after all. *(To* **Edward***)* Your majesty will of course be welcome to my humble bed for the night.

**Edward:** Sleep! What a wonderful thought. But I have no night attire.

**Miles:** Your majesty may be surprised to hear that many of your subjects wear the same clothes from morning to morning, season to season.

**Edward:** Except when they exchange them for the finery of an unsuspecting prince.

**Miles:** You're tired, your majesty. Let me help you.

**Edward:** One thing bothers me.

**Miles:** *(Aside)* One thing!

**Edward:** Of all the people I've met today, only you have even tried to understand. Why is that?

**Miles:** I too know what it is to be denied and disbelieved. *(He picks up lute/guitar and plays)*

**18 Solo: *'Miles Hendon's story'*** (Miles)

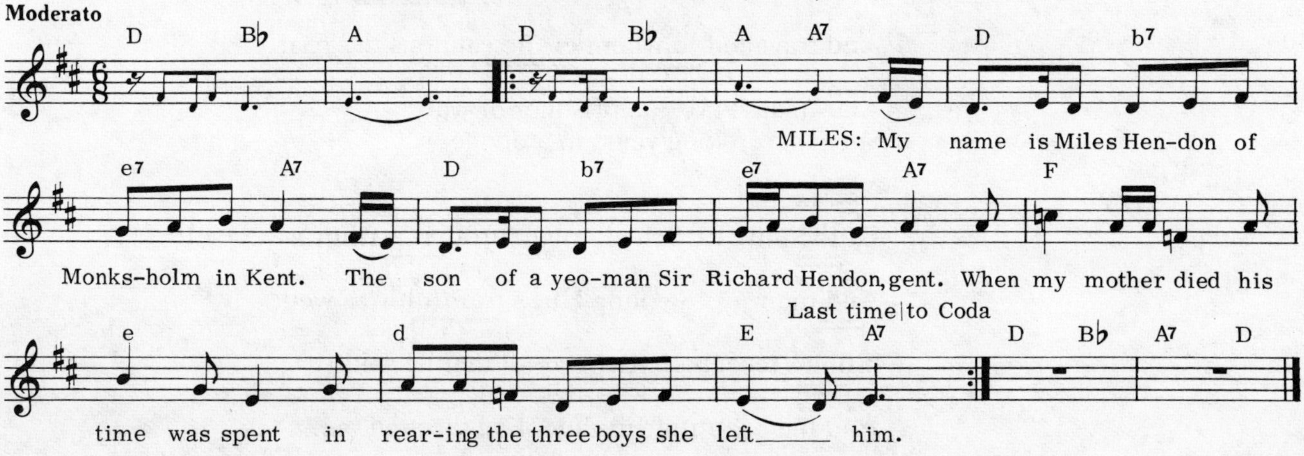

The eldest was Arthur, a kind man, like him;
The youngest was Hugo, his very antonym;
And then there was me, through life I did skim
With never a care for the future.

Then my young cousin Edith came into our care.
She fell for my wildness, I for her beauty, rare;
But my father betrothed her to Arthur, the heir
To all his estates and his fortune.

My father grew old and Arthur fell ill;
And Hugo, ambitious to be first-named in the will,
Set himself to impeach me, his plan to fulfil,
And poisoned my father against me.

One day in my absence he placed 'neath my bed
A strong silken ladder, he afterwards said
I was planning to use to carry off and wed
The beautiful Lady Edith.

My father was sent for and shown the evidence
Of my intended elopement with this child of innocence.
'Three years in the army will teach him some sense',
Said the silver-tongued Hugo to father.

So I went abroad as I told you before,
And travelled to where'er the cannons did roar;
And finally, taken a prisoner of war,
Spent seven long years in a dungeon.

By the time I reached home, brother Arthur was dead
And the wicked young Hugo to Edith was wed.
'I don't recognise you' was all that he said,
And the beautiful Edith looked through me.

He had me expelled from my home and my land.
♬
He called me imposter and he had the upper hand.
So now you know why I understand
♩ ♪ ♩
Your fears and your feelings of helplessness.

*(Song ends. He crosses to* **Edward**, *who has fallen asleep. We cannot see him. He has in fact exited to change into* **Tom** *for the next scene)*

**Miles:** Your majesty? Sleeping like a baby. He's shivering. *(Takes off cape and drapes it over* **Edward***)* Madman or no, he'd benefit from some new clothes. I've little enough money, God knows, but I'd be surprised if I couldn't lay my hands on some cheap material to make him something warmer. Meg!

**Meg:** *(Entering)* Yes, Master Hendon?

**Miles:** Meg, I want you to watch over this poor urchin who's sleeping in my bed.

**Meg:** Who is he?

**Miles:** Good question. But don't ask him, whatever you do. I won't be long.

*(***Miles** *exits)*

# ACT 2 SCENE 9 STATEROOM AT WESTMINSTER

**19 Instrumental: *Fanfare***

*(**Tom** sits on throne upstage. **Hertford** enters)*

**Hertford:** Well, your majesty, how does it feel to be king?

**Tom:** Very strange.

**Hertford:** You'll get used to it.

**Tom:** That's what worries me.

**Hertford:** You will not have to appear in public until the state funeral.

**Tom:** When will that be?

**Hertford:** On the sixteenth of the coming month, my liege.

**Tom:** Next month! Will he keep?

**Hertford:** Your majesty?

**Tom:** In Offal Court we bury our dead within the hour if we can. The plague is always lurking, and if it takes hold . . .

*(**Tom** stops, realising **Hertford** is looking at him strangely)*

**Hertford:** Your majesty will be pleased to hear that your duties for today have been confined to domestic matters.

**Tom:** Duties? Er – what sort of duties?

**Hertford:** Nothing taxing, your majesty. Master Snodgrass and Master Marlow are here to see you.

**Tom:** Who are they?

**Hertford:** The one is your mentor in matters cerebral, the other your surrogate in matters corporal, your majesty.

**Tom:** What does that mean?

**Hertford:** Teacher and whipping boy, my liege.

**Tom:** Whipping boy? What's that?

**Hertford:** Your majesty is still recovering from his recent indisposition. Perhaps your memory will be refreshed when I send them in.

**Tom:** I very much doubt it.

**Hertford:** Will you see them? They seem very concerned about something.

**Tom:** All right.

**Hertford:** Thank you, your majesty.

*(**Hertford** exits, bowing)*

**Tom:** They can't be more concerned than I am.

(Intro to song heralds entrance of **Humphrey Marlow** *and* **Master Snodgrass**. *They bow low with excessive humility)*

**Both:** Good morrow, your majesty.

**Tom:** Good morning – er – gentlemen. What can I do for you?

*(They change in a flash from obsequiousness to supplication, as they go into the song)*

**20 Trio: *'The royal lesson'*** (Tom, Humphrey, Snodgrass)

*(**Tom** steps down from throne)*

**Tom:** I know what a tutor is, but what's a whipping boy?

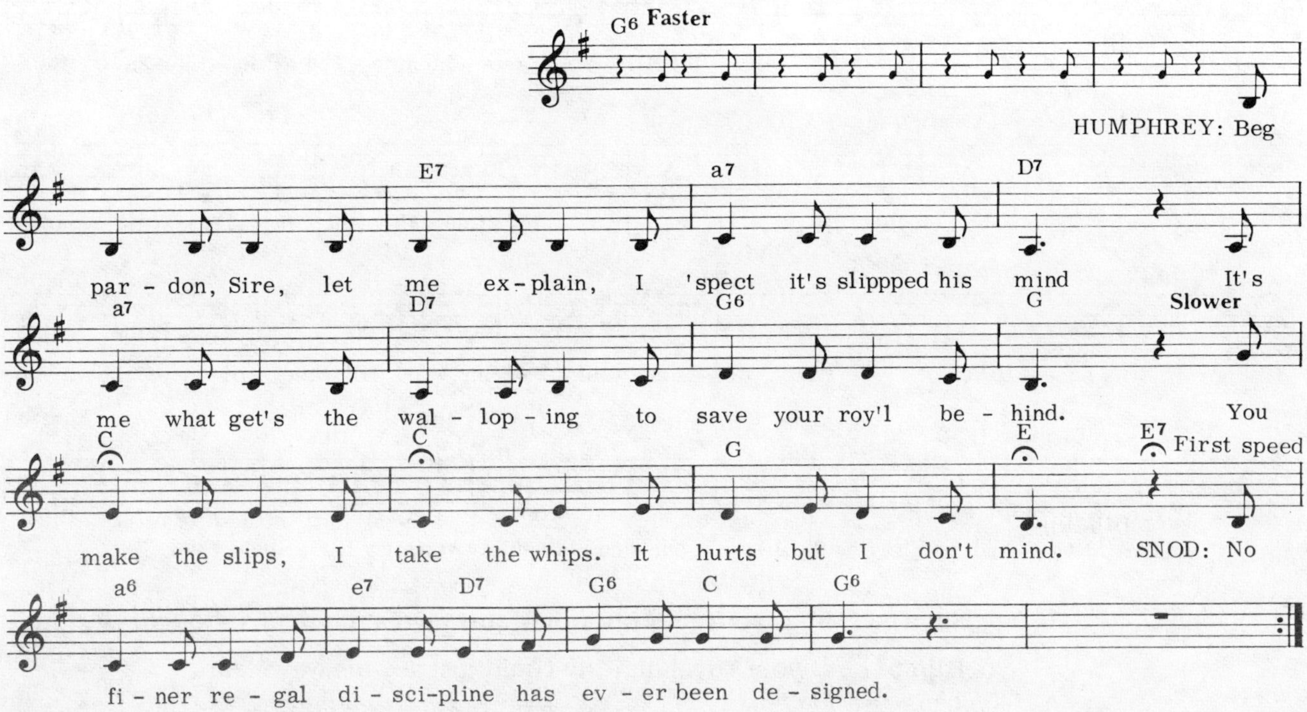

**Tom:** What a strange and curious trade. Now let me get this straight.

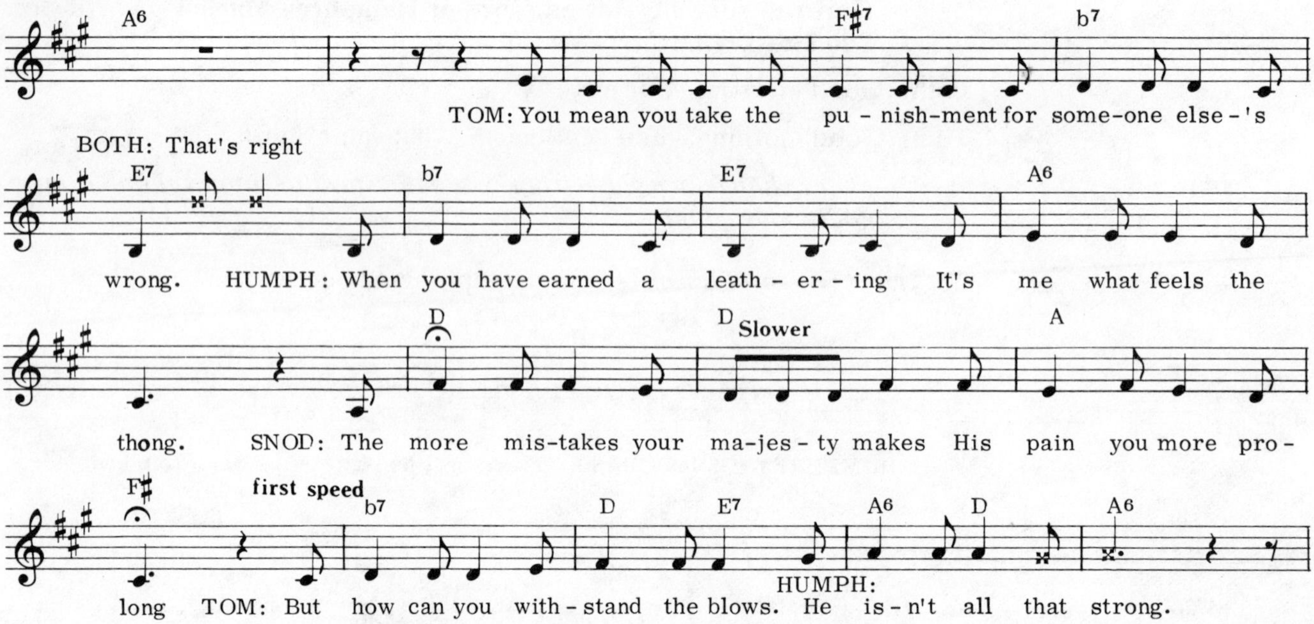


**Tom:** And you are worried about your future?

**Snod:** Exactly so, sire.

**Tom:** Can you tell me why?

**Snod:** Well, sire . . .

**Snod:** So if your majesty would just give a moment's thought . . .
**Hump:** If your royal majesty could just see his way clear to . . .

**Tom:** Silence! *(They shut up and* **Tom** *is stunned by his power)*

**Snod:** *(Spoken)* Well, not exactly, sire, you see . . .

**Tom:** I never heard of such a thing. Can you show me how it works?

**Snod:** Certainly sire. With pleasure. *(At **Hump**)* Or perhaps I should say with pain.

**Hump:** Get on with it.

**Snod:** All right, let's imagine we're in a lesson.

**Hump:** *(Placing chair)* Be seated, sire.

**Snod:** Right, let's see – Ah, yes! Latin!

**Tom:** Oh dear!

Very slow, broken
B F♯7
HUMPH:
SNOD: Canst con-ju-gate a - ma - re Sir. I'm for it if he can't TOM: A - mo, a-mas, a -
B B7 E
-mat. Oh dear SNOD: Hast thou for-got the chant? HUMPH: Here comes the roy - al
(slaps) B G♯ C♯
SNOD:
pun - ish-ment a - ma-mus a - ma-tis a - mant and let that be a
B B6 E B7 E
HUMPH: SNOD: TOM:
les - son, sire And more to come, God grant. Well sire? I sym - pa-thise in
D♯ G♯7 C♯6
H & S: TOM:
ev - 'ry way with your pre-di - ca - ment Yes Yes And so henceforth one
G♯ F♯ B6 E B+7
H & S:
hour a day in this way will be spent Hoo-ray!
Faster
A7
ALL THREE: The tu - tor and the whip - ping boy can
d7 G d7 G7
live and breathe a - gain The King has re - in - sta - ted them and
C6 C7 F
here they will re - main. For e - du - ca - tion's not a thing from
C A7 d7 First speed G7
which one should ab - stain. Since noth - ing in this world can bring such
a a7 F G7 C C6 F G7 C
plea - sure or such pain. ouch!

# ACT 2 SCENE 10 MILES HENDON'S LODGINGS

*(**Miles** enters with bundle of material for **Edward**'s clothes)*

**Miles:** Meg?

*(Draws curtains aside. No **Edward**. Looks around)*

Your majesty? Tom? Meg! Meg!

**Meg:** *(Entering)* Why, Master Hendon. I wasn't expecting you.

**Miles:** Clearly. Where is my young friend?

*(**Meg** looks surprised)*

**Meg:** Did he not find you?

**Miles:** What do you mean?

**Meg:** He went to look for you.

**Miles:** Why would he do that?

**Meg:** Someone came for him. A man. He said you were in trouble.

**Miles:** What did this man look like?

**Meg:** Not the sort you'd want to meet on a dark night.

**Miles:** Canty!

**Meg:** He said his name was Hobbs.

**Miles:** John Canty!

**Meg:** Well, anyway, that's who he's gone off with.

**Miles:** Why? The fool!

**Meg:** He didn't seem to want to. But he was worried about you.

**Miles:** Which way?

**Meg:** I didn't see the going of them, but he did say you were lying wounded in the woods beyond Southwark.

**Miles:** Well, I'm not. But I know someone who will be. And his name isn't Hobbs.

*(**Miles** exits. **Meg** exits. Strike table and chair(s))*

# ACT 2 SCENE 11 IN THE WOODS, OUTSIDE LONDON

*(***John*** and ***Edward*** step into a pool of light)*

**Edward:** Where is Miles Hendon?

**John:** He was lying right there.

**Edward:** Or was it *you* who was lying?

**John:** Well, it got you here, didn't it, eh? *(Grabs* **Edward***)*

**Edward:** Let me go! I might have known.

**John:** That'll teach you to be concerned for others.

**Edward:** He's my one friend in the world.

**John:** Ah, that's where you're wrong, see. Your old dad's seen to that. He's got lots of friends. And his friends are your friends.

*(As he speaks a motley crew of men and women emerge from shadows)*

**Edward:** Who are these people?

**John:** I told you. They're our friends. They're gonna look after you. They're gonna see you don't stray towards the straight and narrow. Right, Master Richard?

*(A lout steps forward)*

**Richard:** Right, Master Canty. *(A gurgling laugh)*

**John:** Hobbs! My name is Hobbs. *(Twists* **Richard***'s arm)* Right?

**Richard:** Right, yeah. Hobbs.

**Edward:** You'll pay dearly for this when I am restored to the throne.

**Man:** Ere, what's he mean?

**John:** I told you he was a bit touched. He's quite normal except he thinks he's the Prince of Wales.

**Man:** King of England, now, don't you mean?

**John:** Yeah. Anyway, it's all a figleaf of his imagination.

*(Enter* **Mrs Canty**, **Nan**, **Bet***)*

**Mrs C:** Tom! What happened?

**Edward:** They tricked me into coming here.

**Nan:** Where's Master Hendon?

**Edward:** God knows. He disappeared.

**John:** *(Sneering)* He went out to buy the boy some clothes.

**Gran:** Hope they fit him all right.

*(The* **Gang** *laughs.* **Edith** *enters and joins Canty ladies)*

**John:** Anyway, come on. Time's a-wasting.

**Bet:** Where we going?

**John:** Southwark. Do a bit o' coney catching.

**Edward:** What's a coney?

**Gran:** A fool. Like you. *(Pokes* **Edward**. **Gang** *laughs)*

**1st Man:** A mug.

**2nd Man:** A charlie.

**3rd Man:** A duffer.

**4th Man:** A pratt.

**John:** All right. All right. Let's go. And Master Richard?

**Richard:** Yessir?

**John:** You look after this boy. Teach him everything you know.

**Richard:** *(With veiled menace)* Right you are, squire. I'll take care of him.

**John:** Come on, then. Let's go an' make some money.

*(The* **Gang** *exits.* **Mrs Canty** *calls after them anxiously)*

**Mrs C:** How long will you be?

*(The girls comfort her in her despair)*

**Edith:** Don't fret. They'll come back. They always do.

**Mrs C:** It's only my poor boy I'm worried about.

**Nan:** He's got a sickness on his brain.

**Bet:** They're taking advantage of him.

**Mrs C:** I don't trust that Richard.

**Edith:** I don't blame you.

**Mrs C:** You don't seem like the others. Are you married to one of them?

**Edith:** No. I've only been here a few weeks.

**Nan:** What brought you here?

**Edith:** Trouble! What else? *(She goes into her song)*

**21 Duet: *'Edith's story'*** (Edith, Miles)

**Bet:** *(After verse 1)* You were an only child?

**Edith:** Yes.

**Mrs C:** You were very privileged.

**Edith:** I was. But it didn't last.

**Nan:** What happened?

**Edith:** *(After verse 2)* Then I went to stay with my uncle.

**Mrs C:** Did he have children?

**Edith:** Three sons.

**Bet:** What were they like?

**Mrs C:** They?

**Edith:** My uncle and his younger son, Hugo.

**Nan:** But why?

**Edith:** The youngest son had plans for me. By the time my love returned from the wars, young Hugo had inherited everything – including me. I was so frightened of what he might do, I denied my love and sent him away. I wish I could have been braver, but my courage failed me.

*(**Miles** has entered during the above and now steps foward)*

**Miles:** You can make up for it now.

**Edith:** Miles! *(Runs into his arms. Song resumes)*

**Miles:** I thought it was Hugo you wanted.

**Edith:** I had to pretend for fear of what he'd do to you.

**Miles:** I'll make him pay for doing that to you. But first I've got to find that boy.

**Mrs C:** He's gone off with his father. *(Pointing)* That way.

E♭ B♭7 E♭ E♭6 B♭7 E♭(sus4) C7 f B♭7 C(sus4) C7
GIRLS: Tho' you go by and by We'll find peace at last, re - cap-ture the past, Those
& EDITH:
& MRS. CANTY:
I must go but by and by, We'll find peace at last, re - cap-ture the past, Those
f c B♭ g C(sus4/2) C f A♭9 B♭7 E♭ C7
hap - py con-ten-ted times that we have longed for, the times that have passed us by.
hap - py con - ten - ted times that we have longed for, the times that have passed us by.
f B♭ E♭ e f7 B♭7 E♭
EDITH & GIRLS: Good - bye.
MILES: Good - bye. MILES & MRS CANTY: Good - bye.

# ACT 2 SCENE 12 STATEROOM AT WESTMINSTER

**22 Instrumental: *'Make way for the Prince'*** (Reprise)

**Storyteller:** So . . .
With Edward still some way from being found
And people of the court so taken in
Young Tom was well and truly on the throne.
*(We see* **Tom** *on throne)*
And though this may seem somewhat hard to swallow
Remember: Tom had played at kings for years.
Not only did he look just like the king
But knew how to behave like him as well
And that's just what the court forced him to do
For them, he *was* the king. His word was law.
And Tom could no more go against their schemes
Than lay his head upon the chopping block.
His royal games had become real games – for now
And he was getting used to it.

*(***Storyteller** *exits)*

*(Enter* **Hertford**, **Executioner**, **Guard**, **Male Prisoner**, **Female Prisoner**, **Fool**, **Courtiers** *in procession.* **Catherine**, **Elizabeth** *and* **Jane** *enter and take positions around the throne during introduction to song)*

**23 Chorus: *'The trial'* (Hertford, Executioner, Two Prisoners, Fool, Catherine, Elizabeth, Jane, Tom)**

**Tom:** Did anyone see the poison given?

**Hertford:** No, my liege.

**Tom:** Was any poison found?

**Guard:** None, your majesty.

**Tom:** And on such lack of evidence you'd send a man to hang?

**Man:** Oh yes, please, your majesty. Let them hang me, I beg of you. Anything but what they have in store for me.

**Tom:** What do you mean?

**Hertford:** Your majesty, this man is to be boiled alive.

**Exec:** *(With relish)* In oil.

**Tom:** Thrown alive into a vat of boiling oil?

**Exec:** Not thrown, your majesty. But hoisted up and lowered bit by bit. Feet first. Tis 'orrible death. *(Chuckles)*

**Tom:** Lord Hertford.

**Hertford:** Your majesty?

**Tom:** You say I am king. Does that mean my word is law?

**Hertford:** *(Hesitant)* It does . . .

**Tom:** In that case, I wish to change the law. So that no man, whatever his crime, shall have to suffer such torment in its name. Can that be done?

**Hertford:** It can be done, your majesty. But due consideration must be given to the . . .

**Tom:** I have considered the *facts*, Lord Hertford. And must confess I find them lacking in conviction.

**Hertford:** But your majesty!

**Tom:** Until stronger evidence is produced this man must go free.

**All:** *(Except* **Hertford** *and* **Female Prisoner***)* Hooray!

*(The following is sung to music as above)*

**Tom:** *(Sings)* Now let us hear the facts behind the case of
This girl for whom the passing bell is soon to toll.

**Hertford:** *(Sings)* She is a witch! She bears the trace of
The Devil with whom she bargained for her soul.

**All:** *(Singing)* Amen!

**Q'tet** *(Singing)* She bargained with the Devil for her soul. The Devil for her soul.

*(The* **Woman** *hurls herself at* **Tom***'s feet)*

**Woman:** *(Spoken)* Your majesty, it isn't true!

**Tom:** *(Sings)* Pray calm yourself, you must have seen
You'll get a proper trial.

**Woman:** *(Sings)* God bless your royal majesty, but I've been treated vile.
They say to raise a storm one night the skies I did beguile.

**All:** *(Singing)* And all she did was take her shoes and socks off.

**Tom:** *(Sings)* Your shoes and socks?

**Woman:** *(Sings)* I took them off to bathe my aching feet.
And by some chance it then began to rain and hail and sleet.

**Hertford:** *(Sings)* And caused a flood that washed away a hamlet and a street.

**All:** *(Singing)* And half the population lost their houses. *(Music stops)*

**Tom:** And did this woman lose her home?

**Guard:** She did, sire.

**Tom:** Not much of a witch, then, was she?

**Exec:** I reckon she played it crafty, to avert suspicion.

**Hertford:** But everyone saw her work the spell.

**Tom:** By taking off her shoes and socks?

**Hertford:** Precisely, your majesty.

**Tom:** All right, then. Good woman – off with your shoes and socks.

*(All panic)*

**Hertford:** But your majesty!

**Tom:** Let's see a storm.

**Exec:** We'll all be drowned!

**Tom:** We'll see.

**Woman:** Oh your majesty, I haven't got the power. I've been falsely accused.

**Tom:** In which case we have nothing to fear – except the wrath of God for judging you so harshly. Take them off.

*(As she does so, all except* **Tom** *take cover, mutter prayers, etc.* **Tom** *looks on as they await the consequences of her action, vainly. At length,* **Hertford** *rises cautiously and feels for rain)*

**Tom:** Rather dry for the time of year, wouldn't you say, Lord Hertford?

**Hertford:** It's a trick.

**Tom:** No trick, Lord Hertford. But justice. She goes free!

**All:** *(Except* **Hertford***)* Hooray!

CATH & ELIZ.
& JANE: What will the ex - e - cu - tion - er do now to earn a crust? EX: My
mask-'ll get the moth I'm sure, my axe-'ll go to rust. ALL: No longer will we cleave to laws so
wick-ed and un - just. Un - less the case is proved be-yond all ques-tion.
Soft shoe shuffle
Suddenly slower (instrumental)
ALL: No more will hap-less pri-son-ers be trans-formed in-to dust
un - less the case is proved, Un - less the case is proved. Un
un - less the case is proved, Un - less the case is proved. Un -
less the case is proved be - yond all ques-tion.
less the case is proved be - yond all ques-tion.

## ACT 2 SCENE 13 A LONDON STREET

*(Enter* **Richard** *carrying a sack. He looks round, warily)*

**Richard:** Come on, then, your majesty. This looks like a good spot for a bit of coney-catching.

**Edward:** What exactly is coney-catching?

**Richard:** Putting one over on people.

**Edward:** I'm none the wiser.

**Richard:** You've got a lot to learn about making a living.

**Edward:** Tell me.

**Richard:** You catch people on their way to market, see. And you say: 'Excuse me sir,' – or madam, as the case may be – 'I've a fine young sucking pig in this here sack, and it's going cheap.'

**Edward:** Let me see.

**Richard:** Ah, that's what they all say. And you say: 'I wouldn't advise that, sir' – or madam,

**Both:** As the case may be –

**Richard:** 'Cos this here's a lively little pig and he'll very likely escape, and then you'll have lost a bargain, won't you?'

*(He fakes a tussle with the sack as if to prove his point)*

That usually gets 'em, cos they're all greedy as pigs, the lot of 'em.

**Edward:** You can let me see, though, can't you?

**Richard:** Course I can. *(Shows briefly and closes quickly)*

**Edward:** That's not a pig. It's a cat.

**Richard:** Ah, but we don't show it to 'em, do we?

**Edward:** But surely, when they open the bag . . .?

**Richard:** They don't do that, though, do they? Not after all we've said about what a lively young blighter he is. Especially when they've paid good money for him. They wait till they get home.

**Edward:** By which time we're long gone.

**Richard:** You catch on fast.

**Edward:** It all sounds too easy.

**Richard:** Believe me, it is. Look out, here comes a likely customer.

*(A foppish* **Gent** *approaches.* **Richard** *accosts him, pausing only to wink at* **Edward***)*

**Richard:** Excuse me, sir. *(Aside)* Or madam as the case may be.

**Fop:** Yes? What is it?

**Richard:** You're on your way to market. Am I right?

**Fop:** Yes I am as it happens. Why?

**Richard:** Well, sir, it just so happens I've a fine young sucking pig in this here sack. And it's going cheap.

**Fop:** *(Licking lips)* Mmm. Really. Let me see it.

**Richard:** *(Tussles with bag)* Oh, I wouldn't advise that, sir. As you can see, he's a lively little chap, and I'm afraid he might escape. And then you'll have missed a bargain, won't you.

**Fop:** Well, I don't know. Without seeing it . . .

**Richard:** Very tender, he is, sir. My colleague here'll vouch for that. *(Silence. So* **Richard** *prompts)* Won't you, Master Thomas?

**Edward:** Oh yes. As pigs go, he's the cat's whiskers.

**Richard:** *(Aside)* Careful, my friend. *(Aloud)* Real bargain, too.

**Fop:** How much?

**Edward:** More than he's worth. You can be sure of that.

**Richard:** Hey! *(With menace)*

**Edward:** Give it here.

*(Grabs bag.* **Richard** *holds on. They struggle)*

**Richard:** Watch it. You'll let the cat out of the bag. *(To* **Fop**, *covering)* Oh my word, he is lively, sir. *(To* **Edward***)* Cut it out, you damn fool.

**Edward:** *(Under)* Did you honestly think I'd be a party to this?

*(The bag has become unimportant in the struggle. It falls to the ground. The* **Fop** *picks it up and examines the contents. We hear a fierce 'miaow' and the* **Fop** *hastily closes the bag. He struggles with it as if the cat is trying to get out. The fight continues)*

**Fop:** This isn't a pig. It's a cat.

*(The fight stops.* **Richard** *feigns innocence)*

**Richard:** No! Let me have a look. *(Looks. Miaow/struggle as before)* Well, I'm blowed.

**Fop:** Don't come the old innocent with me. Cheat! *(Calls offstage)* Help! Felony! Cozenage!

**Richard:** Quick! Run for it.

*(He puts bag into* **Edward***'s hands and dashes off.* **Edward** *dithers)*

**Fop:** *(Returning)* Oh no you don't.

*(He hurls his cloak over* **Edward***'s head and holds him fast.* **Miles** *enters, with a few others)*

**Miles:** What's going on? Do you need help, my friend?

**Fop:** This young devil was trying to sell me a pig in a poke. His accomplice got away, I'm afraid.

**Miles:** Let's have a look at him. *(Removes cloak)* Tom!

**Fop:** You know him?

**Miles:** He's a friend of mine.

**Fop:** *(Suspicious)* Really?

*(Two* **Men** *take positions either side of* **Miles***. One holds a knife to* **Miles'** *throat)*

**Man 1:** Friend of yours, is he, squire?

**Miles:** Yes, he is.

**Man 2:** *(Knife)* You won't mind sharing a cell with him, then, will you?

**Edward:** Leave him alone. He's nothing to do with this.

**Man 1:** *(Grabbing* **Edward***)* That's for the magistrate to decide. Come on.

*(They hustle* **Miles** *and* **Edward** *off, with onlookers in tow)*

## ACT 2 SCENE 14 THE STOCKS

*(Slow drum, building. After a moment or two,* **Storyteller** *enters)*

**Storyteller:** The punishment for cozenage was harsh
Full twenty strokes delivered by the lash
And then a healthy pelting in the stocks
Such was the fate that Miles and Edward faced.
The magistrate looked sternly at the pair,
'And what have you to say in your defence?'
'I am the King of England,' Edward said
And straightaway the court rose to its feet:
'You cannot punish someone who is mad.'
So Edward was allowed to go unpunished.
His only retribution was to be
To see his friend Miles Hendon take the lash
And then humiliation in the stocks.

*(During the last few lines, the lights come up to reveal* **Miles** *near collapse in the stocks. The two* **Men** *enter, holding* **Edward** *between them, in a position where he can see. A crowd gathers silently, the women's heads covered with scarves or shawls. They carry baskets of scraps. Slowly, deliberately, they begin pelting* **Miles***, the drum punctuating their shots, gathering speed. Every missile thrown causes* **Miles** *to shudder in silent agony until, with a mighty scream*

*he stiffens, then falls unconscious. The pelting and drumming stop. The crowd falls silent. They look at* **Miles**, *at each other, then quietly depart. Two men unlock the stocks. Two hurl* **Edward** *to the ground before them)*

**Man 1:** P'raps that'll teach you.

**Man 2:** Here, give him his sword when he wakes up. Though I don't think he'll be using it for a while.

*(Hands* **Miles**' *sword and buckler to* **Edward**. *The men exit, leaving* **Edward** *alone with* **Miles**, *who now stirs, rises to his knees and, freeing his hands from the unlocked stocks, flexes them and stares at them as if to say 'I'd like to use these fists to smash the people who've done this to me.' He then stares at* **Edward**, *who looks on helplessly. There's nothing to be said.* **Edward** *draws the sword and lays it gently on* **Miles**' *shoulder)*

**Edward:** Arise, Sir Miles Hendon.

*(***Miles** *holds* **Edward**'*s gaze for some seconds, then breaks down.* **Edward** *sheaths the sword, helps him up, and they shamble off)*

## ACT 2 SCENE 15 THE CORONATION

*(Two men enter and remove the stocks. Others sweep up the scraps with besoms.* **Storyteller** *enters)*

**Storyteller:** And so the two were free to go to London
And as it happened they were not alone
For everyone, it seemed, was going there
To see the King of England being crowned
The streets were swept and cleared of all obstructions
To give the royal procession right of way
And people came from miles around to witness
The splendour of that Coronation Day.

*(Back tabs open to reveal coronation throne in position)*

**24 Instrumental:** ***'Make way for Edward, Prince of Wales'*** (Reprise)

*(Procession enters with* **Tom** *looking apprehensive, finely robed and accompanied by* **Hertford**, **Catherine**, **Elizabeth**, **Jane** *and peers and peeresses of the realm, the* **Archbishop**, *and the* **Fool** *carrying the crown on a cushion. The Coronation Robe is ceremoniously draped around* **Tom**'*s shoulders. He is led to the throne. The orb and sceptre are placed in his hands. The* **Archbishop** *takes the crown and raises it on high. At the same moment the peers and peeresses raise their coronets and hold them poised over their heads.*

*Music strikes a pregnant chord.*
*A sudden commotion offstage. Two guards back on holding their halberds against someone in the wings we can't see.*
*We hear* **Edward***'s voice offstage, in fact spoken by* **Tom** *from behind the archbishop's robe)*

**Edward:** *(Off)* Get out of my way. I am the king. It's me they should be crowning.

*(The* **Archbishop** *lowers his arms and he and* **Tom** *turn to look offstage)*

**Hertford:** What's happening?

**Guard:** A pauper boy, my lord. He's raving. He says he's the king. *(Spits command into wings)* Hold him!

**Tom:** No. Let him go. He is the King of England. It's me you should be holding.

**Hertford:** Your majesty!

**Tom:** Look at him. Take a good look. Now look at me. Can you not see the resemblance?

**Hertford:** It's uncanny.

**Tom:** Ask him a question. Any question from the many you have put to me that I have failed to answer. And he will answer true. Ask him where the Great Seal of England is kept.

*(***Tom** *steps up to the throne, takes off robe and leaves it there)*

**Hertford:** But he won't know that. Even your majesty has forgotten.

**Tom:** Wrong, Lord Hertford. You thought I'd forgotten. The fact is, I never knew. He does.

*(***Tom** *leaves, abruptly. A stunned silence)*

**Hertford:** After him.

**Edward:** *(Off)* No! Leave him! Your king commands it!

*(***Edward** *pushes the halberds apart and enters. All murmur)*

The Great Seal of England lies in a secret jewel closet in the north wall of the king's ante-chamber. The closet opens when a certain brazen nail-head is pressed. The device was installed by an artisan on the morning of his execution, so that none should learn the secret.

*(They all stare at him in stunned silence)*

Of course, now I've told the world, it'll have to be changed.

**Hertford:** Your majesty!

*(***Hertford** *hurls himself at* **Edward***'s feet. The rest bow low)*

**Peer:** Long live the king!

**All:** Long live the king!

**Hertford:** On with the coronation!

**Edward:** One moment. There is a man outside who should have pride of place here. A man who has put his life at risk for me without question, not knowing who I am. Call Sir Miles Hendon.

*(A buzz of 'never heard of him' remarks)*

**Guard:** Call Sir Miles Hendon.

**Voices:** *(Off, receding)* Call Sir Miles Hendon! Call Sir Miles Hendon!

**Edward:** This man is the only one who took my part, other than the family of the boy who took my place. I intend to reward him with an earldom. And the pauper boy, when he is found, will be granted the honoured title of King's Ward. In his guise I have seen the oppression my people suffer under the law. Ah, Sir Miles.

*(**Miles** enters slowly, disbelief turning to shame. He bows low)*

**Miles:** Your majesty! Can you ever forgive me?

**Edward:** Thanks to you, sir, I shall be the most forgiving king that ever sat on this throne.

**Peer:** Long live the king!

**All:** Long live the king!

*(As **Edward** is regaled for the coronation)*

**25 Chorus: *'Long live the king!'*** (Full company)

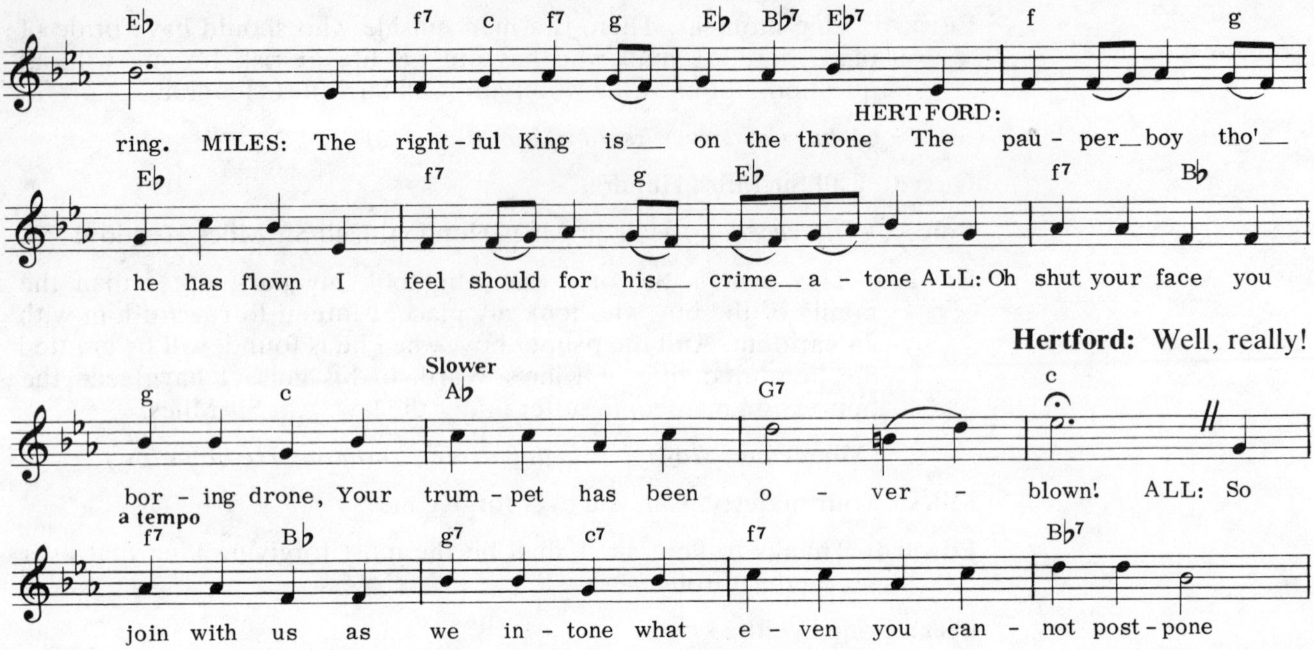


**(Storyteller** *speaks over music while cast sing melody to 'la'. Action freezes)*

*(Action freezes, dialogue over music)*

**Storyteller:** *(Spoken)* Tom Canty lived to be a grand old man.
His mother and his sisters prospered with him.
His father? No one heard of him again.
Miles Hendon was created Earl of Kent.
His properties and lands were all restored,
As was his well-beloved Lady Edith,
His brother, spared the gallows by the king,
Was banished for his wicked treachery,
And died soon after that, a sorry man.
And Edward, though his life was short, became
A king of England worthy of the name.

*(Cast sing last verse)*

*End of Act Two*